What a Mighty God!

135 Life Lessons

Inspirational Devotions, Poems and Stories

For I am convinced that neither death nor life, neither angels nor demons, neither the present nor the future, nor any powers, neither height nor depth, nor anything else in all creation, will be able to separate us from the love of God that is in Christ Jesus our Lord.

Romans 8:38-39

by

Marilyn Phillips and Rebekah Phillips

with

articles and poems from 14 contributors

Acknowledgments

Special thanks to Nolan Phillips for editing and formatting this book. Nolan has taught adult Bible studies for over 41 years and was our advisor on this project. I couldn't have written this book without him!

Special thanks to Barbara Christa who is my mentor. She has encouraged and prayed with me during the writing of this book.

Contents

Fruit of the Spirit

God's Plans

God's Directions

God's Provisions

Choices

God's Faihtfullness

Actions

Ministry

Heaven and Eternity

SALVATION

For it is by grace you have been saved, through faith -- and this not from yourselves, it is the gift of God, not by works, so that no one can boast.
Ephesians 2:8-9

1 ✟ CREATED BY GOD

For you created my inmost being; you knit me together in my mother's womb.
Psalms 139:13

My mother, Mary Kathryn White, was ninety years old this year and our family had a huge celebration including her favorite cake and food. We presented a slide show that represented highlights of her life. I share this special day because I was born on my mom's birthday so we celebrate the occasion together! That makes the day even more meaningful for me.

Isn't it exciting to celebrate your birthday! Family and friends focus on you for the entire day and you receive gifts as all celebrate the day you were born. My family takes me to my favorite restaurant. My friends treat me to lunch and I receive inspirational cards. I delight each time I open a gift or card that was purchased specifically for me.

But can you see the bigger picture? Did you know that your birthday was planned by God long before it actually occurred? Not only that, but also God created a unique "you" to do specific ministry? The talents and gifts He gave you prepare you to minister to others in your life.

Our daily decisions influence the people God puts in our lives. We were created by God to glorify Him in all we do.

Do you visualize yourself as God's child before you speak or act? How will this influence what you say or do each day?

✟   Marilyn Phillips

2 ✝ WHEN GOD CREATED YOU

The angels are watching, the day has come.
God said, "It is good, your life has begun."
God was full of inspiration,
When He began your creation.

He had a plan for you before your birth,
Before you made your appearance on earth.
You would have to be special,
Everything about you would be crucial.

God was anxious as your life began,
To see His creation live His plan.
God knows the choices you will make,
And has equipped you for the steps you will take.

Learning important instructions on living is vital,
So read God's love letter to you, the Bible.
You are called to believe in Jesus; and of bad choices repent,
Then make good choices and live your life as God meant.

Even when the choices don't go as they should,
God will work them out for good.
Jesus has whispered to you today,
Follow me, I will make a way.

So, my friend, I say with great affection,
You are one of a kind, God's special creation.

✝   ©Beth Peery

3 ✞ SIN

For all have sinned and fall short of the glory of God and are justified freely by his grace through the redemption that came by Christ Jesus.
Romans 3:23-24

What is sin? It is any thought or action that separates us from God. In fact, Habakkuk 1:13 states that God's *eyes are too pure to look on evil …* so, to stay in fellowship with God, we must learn to recognize sin in our lives.

Basically, sin is doing things our way instead of God's way. The first step to understanding sin is to know what the Bible says about it. God laid out His basic principles of life in the Ten Commandments. Do you know where to find the Ten Commandments in the Bible? They are found in Exodus 20:1-17. Jesus made the commandments even stricter when He said it was sin when we even think about violating them. Jesus also summarized them into two basic principles: love God, and love others as yourself.

God provided His commandments to show how to live a full life that honors Him in all we say and do. Each of us fail to keep the commandments, so it was necessary for God to provide another way.

Jesus paid the penalty for your sin and my sin that we might live through Him.

Do you understand that you are a sinner and that God provided a Savior in Christ Jesus for you?

✞   Marilyn Phillips

4 ✞ FORGIVENESS

As far as the east is from the west, so far has he removed our transgressions from us.
Psalms 103:12

Have you ever thought about eternity and how long it will last? Eternity is real, and we all will exist forever. However, our destination in eternity is a choice.

We can believe in God, trust in His provision for covering and forgiving our sin, and spend eternity in heaven, or refuse to believe, reject His provision, and let our destination be eternal separation from God. Sin separates us from God.

We all have sinned. God gives us the promise that our sins will be forgiven and forgotten. When you confess your sins and trust in His provision, God forgives.

Jesus died on the cross to pay for every sin that you or I have ever committed in the past and every sin that we will commit in the future. The Bible has a promise about forgiveness in I John 1:9, *"If we confess our sins, He is faithful and just and will forgive us our sins and purify us from all unrighteousness."*

You might be thinking that your sins aren't as bad as others. For instance, you have never murdered anyone. But in God's eyes, all sins are transgressions of His Law. Jesus said that one is guilty of all if she is guilty of any.

Have you trusted in Jesus as God's provision for your sin?

✞   Marilyn Phillips

5 ✞ GOD'S GRACE

For it is by grace you have been saved, through faith - and this not from yourselves, it is the gift of God, not by works, so that no one can boast.
Ephesians 2:8-9

Is there anything that we can do to earn salvation? No, there is nothing that you can do to pay for your sin. Earning salvation is like trying to swim from Los Angeles to Hawaii. An Olympic swimmer might make it much further than we could, but we all would fail to reach the goal of arriving on the shores of Hawaii. In the same way, we can never be good enough to earn our way to Heaven.

Salvation is a gift from God. It came at a great price which was the death of Jesus Christ. Salvation is yours if you have repented of your sins and asked Christ to be your Lord and Saviour.

You will never be good enough to earn your own salvation … remember, if you are guilty of one sin, you are guilty of all. The classic example of this is the answer to the question, "How many rotten eggs does it take to spoil the whole omelet?" Well, just one bad egg is enough! It's the same principle with sin.

There isn't anything that you can do to deserve salvation – the requirement is absolute perfection. Salvation is a Gift from God. He offers us the perfection of Jesus in exchange for all of our failures. Pretty good deal!

Have you received the gift of salvation?

✞   Marilyn Phillips

6 ✟ THE DAY I WAS SAVED

"You better shape up!" my best friend said,
Oh! I'm so crushed! Thoughts race through my head!
How could she think my holier than thou attitude was bad?
It's okay if I tell her my husband made me mad.
He didn't want to go to church that night,
I just didn't think that was right!
On the way home from church, flooded with such hurt, I cry,
God was leading me to take the plank out of my eye.
My uncontrollable crying forced me to stop in the parking lot,
That was where God got my attention – my life was finally bought.
When I was ten, I said I believed in Jesus and was baptized,
All the time I had not realized that I was not saved!
The sin in my life had me enslaved.
At ten, what was repentance and sin?
I don't kill, steal, or lie was my thinking within.
On church attendance, and works I could no longer rely,
My life couldn't be bought no matter how hard I tried.
I studied the Bible, searched, listened, and learned,
But did not know something was left unearned.
I never earned the right to know Jesus as my Savior,
Did not know that complete surrender was the behavior.
This was a divine appointment, I have no doubt!
From that tomb of sin I was about to break out!
God knew about that moment before I was born,
I surrendered and said, "I can't do this without You." And was reborn!
I said, "I am so sorry, please forgive me for my sins."
"Guide me – Jesus, be the Lord of my life,"
and this is where my new life begins.
The complete surrender feels good.
God's words in the Bible are now understood.
Even though new life begins, It doesn't mean I never sin,
But with the Holy Spirit within, I won't be ignorant of my sins.
When I ask God for forgiveness and turn away,
The Holy Spirit convicts and I want to obey.

✟   ©Beth Peery

7 ✝ SALVATION

Then I will tell them plainly, "I never knew you.
Away from me, you evildoers!"
Matthew 7:23

During the summer of my ninth grade, my high school cheer team went to a church service each night at a Christian Cheerleaders of America camp. One night, a cheerleader coach gave a dynamic testimony. As a youth, she had attended all the church functions and knew much about God and the Bible, but a personal relationship with God was lacking. Therefore she was going to spend an eternity in hell. Realizing that she didn't know God, she immediately fell to her knees and asked forgiveness and asked God to come into her heart.

That day an inner peace came to this teenager as a result of her new relationship with God. This testimony described me. I grew up in a Christian home, went to a Christian school and had parents that loved the Lord. Somehow, I had convinced myself that I was going to heaven because I knew the right answers and did Christian things.

I finally understood what was missing in my life! I accepted that I needed a personal relationship with my Savior! I almost missed knowing God! He wanted me to hear this testimony! Immediately, I had an inner peace that this world cannot give.

Do you have this peace? Do you really know God?

✝ Rebekah Phillips

8 ☦ SIN TAKEN AWAY

We all, like sheep, have gone astray, each of us has turned to his own way; and the LORD has laid on him the iniquity of us all.
Isaiah 53:6

It is easy for us to identify with the sheep that have gone astray. We can all recall things from our past wherein we have failed. However, for some of us it is much more difficult to believe that Jesus has actually taken those things away ... forever.

Sometimes we still want to hang on to our guilt, not believing that God really did lay our iniquity onto His Son, Jesus Christ.

Satan likes to trap us by constantly reminding us of our sinful past and by making us feel guilty and unworthy of a relationship with Jesus.

Can you see your sins nailed to the cross? Jesus truly has borne the price for sin and removed them. In Psalm 102:11-12, it promises, "For as high as the heavens are above the earth, so great is his love for those who fear him; as far as the east is from the west, so far has he removed our transgressions from us."

Have you thanked God and given Him praise for this great gift of salvation?

☦   Marilyn Phillips

9 ✞ THE LIGHT

The sun peeks over the horizon and light floods the earth,

Slowly, everything appears to have a new birth.

The earth seems to have been washed clean,

By the heaven-sent, dewy sheen.

Cool air flows into our body with a rush,

As if a breath from heaven came down like a hush.

The light flows into our souls also,

Replacing the darkness we have come to know.

Our sins are washed away,

As the flood of light has its way.

The breath of life pours in and as we come alive,

Our dead soul begins to revive.

This life-giving decision is ours to make,

Our whole eternity is at stake.

You ask, what must I do? What must I say?

Jesus, the Light of the World, is the only way.

He's the One who died on a cross to take your sin,

Thus allowing your new life to begin.

You must confess your sins; ask God to forgive you,

Telling Jesus you can't live your life without Him you now should do.

Now your sin barrier is removed,

And your relationship with God is approved.

Live your life seeking His will for you,

Read God's word, pray, and listen to Him speak to you.

Turning from sin isn't easy some days,

Just keep your eyes on Jesus, He will make a way.

✞   ©Beth Peery

10 ✞ 911 CALLS ON 9/11

For God so loved the world that he gave his one and only Son, that whoever believes in him shall not perish but have eternal life.
John 3:16

I was enjoying my daily walk where I could experience the dawning of a new day. Stopping at the small pond in the park near my home, I prayed about life's frustrations knowing that God listened. Upon my return, I clicked on the TV. To my astonishment and dismay, there were pictures of a tremendous fire raging in New York. What could have happened? Suddenly, an airplane crashed into the next tower. This image was etched forever in my mind. Horror stricken, I prayed for the people trapped inside.

News crews scrambled for facts. They reported planes had hit both World Trade Center Towers and the Pentagon. However, nothing made sense. Frantic calls to 911 were reportedly made from those inside the buildings proclaiming the hopelessness of no escape and certain death.

Everyone knows that when you make a 911 call that HELP will be immediately on the way. But, no one could help those in the planes or burning buildings that tragic day.

Cameras showed hundreds of courageous firemen and police officers running to the building. Fire and smoke engulfed the sky. Suddenly the buildings crumbled. They just collapsed before my eyes. Tons of steel and concrete, like an avalanche, rushed to the ground and formed a great dust storm. Uncontrollable tears racked my body. The people … what happened to all of the people? Thousands were praying at that precise moment.

Surely, there would be many discovered in the rubble. But after several days when few were found alive ... hope for survivors seemed lost.

Did the 911 calls mean nothing? What about our prayers? Had they gone unheard? The events were traumatic and the nation was transfixed on the TV for any glimpse of hope.

I lay awake at night with vivid images of the plane crashing into the tower, firemen rushing to their death, and buildings crumbling ... some people even jumped from burning buildings to their death.

Did God even hear our desperate prayers and 911 calls? Many grabbed a phone and dialed 911 upon realizing that there was an immediate danger and people were trapped and couldn't save themselves. Firemen were unable to help those trapped in the burning buildings that day.

I searched for more answers and I found them in the Bible which is the source of promise. Eternal life was waiting for all on that day who believed the Bible, *"And this is the testimony: God has given us eternal life, and this life is in His Son. He who has the Son has life; he who does not have the Son of God does not have life. "* (I John 5:11-12)

I still wondered, "Did some make a last minute plea to God?" If so, God promises that they were ushered into Heaven. *"Call unto me, and I will answer you and tell you great and unsearchable things you do not know."* (Jeremiah 33:3) In Revelation 21, we read about a glorious Heaven beyond belief with streets of gold where there are no more tears, pain, mourning or death.

For Christians, God has a 911 number, Psalm 91:1. *"He who dwells in the shelter of the Most High will rest in the shadow of the Almighty. I will say of the Lord, He is my refuge and my fortress, my God, in whom I trust."*

God is waiting and ready for your 911 call. He will answer.

I still take a daily walk. Now, I have more appreciation for beauty and the miracle of life. Since that eventful day, I feel an urgency to share about the hope I have in Christ.

Our entire nation will never be the same since the horrific events that led to the 911 calls on September 11th.

Lives are changed forever once the 911 call is made to God.

Have you made a 911 call to God?

✝   Marilyn Phillips

GOD
AT WORK
IN YOUR LIFE

Be still, and know that I am God.

Psalms 46:10a

11 ✞ BUT WHAT ABOUT YOU?

But what about you? Who do you say I am?

The holy words echo through the ages
In a persistent whisper from the ancient pages.

The still small voice is not a dream or your imagination,
It is an invitation from the God of all creation!

You won't be able to see Him with your eyes.
But He is there; there is no disguise.

He is in the rain falling gently on the trees,
You can feel Him In the warm summer breeze.

You can see Him in mountains rising from the sea.
And in birds flying unfettered and free.

You can hear Him in leaves blowing in the wind,
And in children's laughter that has no end.

All of creation declares His love
Sent from the Father of lights from above.

He is through all and in all!
Do you hear the persistent call?

But what about you? Who do you say I am?
Read Luke 9:20

✞   ©Beth Peery

12 ✟ QUIET TIME WITH GOD

For God is not a God of disorder but of peace.
1 Corinthians 14:33a

Isn't life so stressful? It's extremely difficult to handle all of the demands on our time. Sometimes we are distracted and just don't feel peace every day. But, peace is available. God is a God of peace.

So, how do you get the peace that God offers? God's peace only comes through a relationship with Him. We must spend time with God each day. Do you have a quiet time when you can read the Bible and pray?

Remember, praying is just talking to God and listening for His response. Many times, I find that His response comes to me as the Holy Spirit speaks to me in a still quiet voice while I am reading His Word. Try keeping a notebook by your Bible so you can write down the Scriptures that God uses to touch your heart.

Perhaps you don't even know how to have a quiet time. It is really simple. Find a place and time when you won't be interrupted (no TV, radio, loud music or other distractions). Focus on getting quiet before God. Read a selection from Scripture. Visualize what the Bible is telling you. Pray (just talk to God as you would a friend) and then, most important, listen!

Will you make time on a daily basis to have a quiet time with God?

✟　　Marilyn Phillips

13 ✞ GUARD YOUR HEART

And the peace of God, which transcends all understanding, will guard your hearts and your minds in Christ Jesus.
Philippians 4:7

Scripture challenges us to "guard your hearts and minds in Christ Jesus." Have you ever thought about this Scripture and what it actually means to you?

How can you "guard your heart" and your mind? We guard and protect things of great value. Do you value your heart and mind?

There are practical ways daily to consider. Do you limit the things you watch on TV? What kind of movies do you watch? When you listen to music, is it uplifting God's message to your heart? What kind of books do you read? Are you wasting your time, or are you choosing music, TV shows, books, and movies that will be worthy of your time?

The Bible says what we see affects us. *Your eye is the lamp of your body. When your eyes are good, your whole body also is full of light. But when they are bad, your body also is full of darkness.* (Luke 11:34).

The way to peace is to guard or protect your heart and keep your mind focused on Jesus.

 How did you guard your heart today?

✞   Marilyn Phillips

14 ✟ PROTECTION

See, I have engraved you on the palms of my [God's] hands; your walls are ever before me.
Isaiah 49:16

I have a beautiful engraved silver frame that I received as a gift from one of the varsity cheerleading teams that I coached.   This frame is in a prominent place on my bookshelf. I loved these amazing cheerleaders. Each girl had unique talents and skills which made them so very special to me. The engraved message on the frame reminds me of the individual team members. The words are permanently etched into the frame and cannot be removed.

Did you know that Scripture says that you are engraved on the palms of God's hands. Just like the names on my silver frame, you will not be removed or un-engraved.

The second thought of this Scripture in Isaiah 49:16 is that God will not remove His eyes from us. The "walls" represent the walls of Jerusalem and by comparison, our lives, but Jesus said, *And surely I am with you always, to the very end of the age.* (Matthew 28:20b)

What does that mean to you? I think it means that for the rest of your life you will not be removed from the power of God's hands or from His watchful eye. Does this make a difference to you?

✟   Marilyn Phillips

15 ✞ GOD'S POWER

Now to him who is able to do immeasurably more than all we ask or imagine, according to his power that is at work within us.
Ephesians 3:20

Are there specific times in your life where you are overwhelmed with God's power at work within you? Has God answered a prayer in a way that can only be explained by, "It's God's power?"

There was a time when I had to have radiation five times a week for six weeks due to breast cancer. It was frightening and overwhelmed me with fear. I was in a large room and positioned on a table where the radiation was aimed directly at the cancer site. The technician would step out of the room and talk to me over a loud speaker as the radiation was administered.

As I lay on the table, tears streamed down my face. Unable to move, I felt hopeless and alone … so I prayed. Instantly, I felt God's presence and knew God would give me the strength and courage to endure radiation treatments.

Has God given you power to succeed in a situation when you couldn't imagine success without Him? Did you feel God's power at work within you? What does this experience tell you about the things that you are facing today?

✞   Marilyn Phillips

16 ✞ PEACE

May the God of hope fill you with all joy and peace as you trust in him, so that you may overflow with hope by the power of the Holy Spirit.
Romans 15:13

Have you ever been in a situation where you felt hopeless? I have and I felt overwhelmed. I had no peace or joy in the situation.

Not long ago, my daughter was in the hospital and due to an extreme adverse reaction to two antibiotic drugs, her kidneys began to fail. I felt hopeless as the kidney functions decreased. Daily, the news from the medical staff was worse and my daughter was close to needing kidney dialysis.

Many were praying for Rebekah. There wasn't anything that I could do to help my daughter. In prayer, I gave the situation to God, and an amazing thing happened … peace came! And, I was able to face the situation.

My daughter's kidneys slowly began to improve and within six weeks, she completely recovered. I praise God for the peace that passes all understanding. (Philippians 4:7)

Have you ever released your tough trials to Him? What did it do for your faith?

Do you have peace from God today?

✞ Marilyn Phillips

17 ✞ IT'S ME, LORD

It's me, Lord, once again,
Trying to give it to you, trying to get rid of the emotional pain.

How many times do I do this?
Over and over, there must be something amiss!

I trust you, I do,
Lord, You say You will see me through.

There have been many times before,
You have taken care of things and then more.

What is different now?
Please help me, tell me how.

Is this why you say to pray without ceasing?
So the focus on my pain will begin decreasing.

I understand, Lord, focus on You and Your Word,
So Your goodness and the world won't become blurred.

Lord, You are the only truth, the only One to trust,
My thoughts and time must readjust.

Please forgive me, Lord, let me start afresh today,
I'm still learning to trust and obey.

✞   ©Beth Peery

18 ✞ HOPE

May your unfailing love rest upon us, O LORD,
even as we put our hope in you.
Psalms 33:22

Have you ever seen God's intervention in your life? I have and it is overwhelming!

There are many instances where God has intervened and directed my path. For instance, when my daughter was three months old, she was diagnosed with Cystic Fibrosis (CF). Doctors said that Rebekah would probably not live beyond age thirteen due to this incurable and progressive disease. I couldn't put my hope in doctors for her future. So, I put my hope in the Lord.

God has directly intervened and miraculously restored Rebekah when her lung functions were dangerously low. She was a cheerleader in high school and received a national award at cheer camp. Rebekah is now a college graduate and a teacher. God has a plan for her life and we praise our mighty God for his intervention.

All of us at some point will experience what we think is a hopeless situation. We must realize that our hope is in God.

When things seem hopeless where do you turn? Will you place your hope in God today?

✞   Marilyn Phillips

19 ✞ BLESSINGS

Blessed are those who are persecuted because of righteousness, for theirs is the kingdom of heaven.
Matthew 5:10

The book, *The Heavenly Man*, by Brother Yun and Paul Hattaway, details the dramatic years that Brother Yun spent in a Chinese prison for the crime of preaching and sharing his faith in God.   This is a dramatic and true story. It is extremely difficult to read because the book details brutal consequences for sharing faith in China.

While in prison, Brother Yun received severe beatings and cruel treatment from the guards for years.   But, God protected Brother Yun and he was miraculously released. Brother Yun returned to preaching and is alive today.

Sometimes our trials seem insurmountable, but when we read the testimony of saints that have endured great hardship, it puts our trials in perspective. If they can make it through these difficult things, then I know God will see me through my trials.

Are you walking through challenges today because of your faith?   God blessed Brother Yun daily even when the situation seemed hopeless.

Do you believe that God will bless you through trials?

✞   Marilyn Phillips

20 ✞ BE STILL

Be still, and know that I am God.
Psalms 46:10a

Have you ever noticed how noisy it is everywhere? Restaurants sometimes have the music so loud that conversations at the table can't even be heard. Most drivers have the radio blaring loud music in the car. At home, the television has the volume on LOUD. It's difficult to focus on God with so much noise.

God wants us to spend alone time with Him. In 1 Kings 19:12, God says He speaks in a *"gentle whisper."* We must listen closely to hear what God is saying. We need to intentionally prepare our hearts to listen.

At times we need to be still in our quiet time before God, but other times we need to be still in our lives while waiting for God's answer. Being still before God is not the same as doing nothing. While being still you must do all the things that God has already instructed you to do.

Did you ever notice how we intentionally plan to have time with those we care about. It is the same with God. Do you have an intentional quiet time with God?

Have you been still before God today in a quiet place so you can receive a message from Him?

✞   Marilyn Phillips

21 ✟ MY PURPOSE

I want to be like Jesus,
To serve Him every day.
To be a beacon shining,
Who lights up others' ways.

Who shows them where to put their feet,
Who shows life at its height,
Who shows my strength is NOTHING,
While I live STRONG IN HIS MIGHT!

I want to show my Savior,
Through my daily walk on earth.
That others would desire His life,
And come to have new birth.

✟   ©Barbara Christa

MY TASK

What is my task that You've designed, What is it I'm to do?
Am I to share, am I to serve, Or just enjoy the view?

Am I do DIE TO SELF and find The path You'd have me walk?
Or am I to PLAY at loving with COMMITMENT that's just TALK?

I must decide, for life is short, My days are numbered few.
SHALL MY LIFE COUNT AND BE THE LIGHT THAT POINTS THIS
WORLD TO YOU?

✟   ©Barbara Christa

22 ✝ GOD WORKS

And we know that in all things God works for the good of those who love him, who have been called according to his purpose.
Romans 8:28

We know that all things in our life are not good. But if we focus on God and look to see how God is working in our lives, we can see things from a different perspective.

Note the key words and phrases in this verse:
- All things – so what is not covered here? Nothing!
- God works [some translations read "God causes to work"] – Who is working? Almighty God!
- For good – what is good? Jesus said only God is good (Matthew 19), therefore good flows from God.

Notice that the verse also has conditions: It is for those (1) who love Him and (2) are called according to His purpose – So, since Christians love God then Christians are called.

Are you seeing events in your life as an inconvenience or do you consider that God has a purpose for your trials?

What trials are you facing today? Can you see God at work in your life?

✝   Marilyn Phillips

23 ✟ TEMPTATION

No temptation has seized you except what is common to man. And God is faithful; He will not let you be tempted beyond what you can bear. But when you are tempted, He will also provide a way out so that you can stand up under it.
1 Corinthians 10:13

When you are in a public room (like a school, theater or a church), there is always an EXIT sign to designate a door for your escape in case of an emergency. Do you know that God has promised that He will always provide a way of escape when you are tempted?

One of my favorite pastors, Craig Etheredge, shared in a sermon that God doesn't provide an EXIT just sometimes, but God promises that there will be an EXIT 100% of the time … yes, every single time. For instance, if you are with a group of friends or co-workers who have decided to do an activity that you know is wrong … you do not have to join.

God has given you the power to LEAVE the group or EXIT and not participate. When tempted by some things, God says the way of escape is just to run – *"flee from sexual immorality"* (1 Corinthians 6:18).

What temptations are you facing today? Are you ready to look for the EXIT that God has already provided for you?

✟   Marilyn Phillips

24 ✝ POWER

O LORD, you are my God, I will exalt you and praise your name, for in perfect faithfulness you have done marvelous things, things planned long ago.

Isaiah 25:1

At times, life gets overwhelming ... just overwhelming! Our commitments can keep us so busy that we can't see God at work in our lives – demands at work and family issues get in the way of focusing on God.

When you feel overwhelmed, do you want to just curl up in a ball and hide? God has given you the power to do the tasks that He has for you. Take a daily TIME OUT so you can have a consistent time with God. You will be amazed!

We must realize that there is enough time in each day to do those things to which God has called us to do. The challenge is to discern what action needs to be taken.

As you spend time with God you will better know His will. Do you understand that God has planned for your life more than you can possibly imagine?

Are you listening to God today?

✝   Marilyn Phillips

25 ✟ NEEDS VERSUS WANTS

***And my God will meet all your needs according to
his glorious riches in Christ Jesus.***
Philippians 4:19

Not long ago, I was at a store and I encountered a mother
with her young daughter. The child was trying to convince
her mom that she REALLY wanted a specific item. However,
the mom adamantly replied, "You don't need that toy!"

It's easy to confuse needs and wants! A want is an item that
is not really necessary. For instance, purchasing the newest
fashion jeans or the name brand purse isn't a need. A need
is something that will sustain your existence - like food,
clothes, water and shelter.

God has promised to provide all of your needs … not your
wants. Here's a suggestion for an activity to help distinguish
between needs and wants. Make one list of ten things you
really need. Now, make another list with your top ten
wants. Evaluate your needs to see if they are really wants.
Compare the two lists. Next, ask God to supply your needs,
and then truly surrender your wants to Him. Trust God to
supply all you need to make you joyful.

Will you praise God today for the needs, and gifts, that He
has so richly provided for you?

✟   Marilyn Phillips

26 ✝ GOD'S FLOW

For it is by grace you have been saved, through faith--and this not from yourselves, it is the gift of God -- not by works, so that no one can boast.
Ephesians 2:8-9

"It's for you." Mama handed me the phone. "This is Happy Hal and you've been chosen to guess the secret toy of the day."

I rolled my eyes at Mama. "I know the answer to the question! It's a transistor radio, but I know it's you, Teddy."

My brother played tricks often. But, this time it was not my brother, it was for real! I squealed and danced a happy dance, but not before I chose an above ground swimming pool as my prize.

The pool made for great fun that summer. One of our favorite water games was running in a circle to stir the waters into a whirlpool. After floating in the current for a few minutes, we'd repeat, and the cycle continued until our fingers wrinkled.

That's very different than the "Lazy River" water park attractions of today. The current flows without any one stirring the water. Another force moves it. There's nothing required to enjoy the flow. Every movement is easier than in still water.

I used to think faith was like our little pool. I thought I had to stir it up. But, no one in the Bible had to work up faith. They either had it or they doubted.

In Mark 9, Jesus descended the mountain after His transfiguration to find his disciples trying unsuccessfully to cast a demon out of a boy, though they'd cast out many demons in Jesus' name.

What happened to their faith? Jesus told them this faith only comes out through prayer. It wasn't a stirring, but a plugging in, a returning to the source of the flow.

When Christ cast out the demon, He used His own faith. In Ephesians 2, Paul explained our faith is a gift.

In Hebrews 12:2, Jesus is called the author and finisher of our faith. Christ originates our faith and completes it. Jesus is our faith.

As believers, we've been given the gift of faith. Daily, we have the privilege of stepping into the flow, praying in faith, and living in courage. Stay ready. It's not a "Lazy River." It's a whirlpool of power.

Have you received God's grace through faith?

Prayer:
Almighty God, Help us stay plugged into your flow.

✝   Tamara Roberts

27 ✞ HOPELESSNESS

But as for me, I will always have hope; I will praise you more and more.

Psalms 71:14

Have you ever been in a situation that seemed hopeless? I have. When the doctor told me that I had breast cancer, I thought my life would end. I felt hopeless, I thought I could never have hope again.. In fact, I didn't think that I could walk to the car after receiving this devastating news. So, my husband and I sat down on a bench in the hallway, cried and prayed. When we prayed, I immediately felt the hope that only comes from God.

So what is hope? Hope is related to the confident assurance we have in God. I knew that even if I died, that my hope was in God. I prayed at that moment of hopelessness for God's will in my life. And, I praised God for the peace.

Do you have hope (confident assurance) in God when faced with a hopeless situation? Or, maybe your situation isn't altogether hopeless, you just need to make it through this day and then throughout tomorrow.

The assurance God gives is the same no matter how big, or how small, the challenge that you are facing.

Do you have hope from God today regardless of the situation in your life?

✞   Marilyn Phillips

28 ✝ JESUS NEVER CHANGES

Jesus Christ is the same yesterday, today, and forever.
Hebrews 13:8

I surrendered my heart to Jesus Christ to be my Savior and Lord when I was only seven years old. God revealed to me through Scripture that I was a sinner (even at age seven) and I repented of my sins and asked Christ to forgive me. I was baptized the next week. I have never doubted that I have eternal life and that God's Holy Bible is true.

When I encounter a difficult situation, I know that the God who saved me many years ago is the same God who is with me today, tomorrow, and will be with me throughout eternity.

I understand that since I trusted God for my eternal destination that I can trust God with the problems of today.

When I was diagnosed with breast cancer, He made Himself so real to me. Each time that I was fearful, I prayed and received peace. I knew that God was BIGGER than any battle that I would ever face including cancer. God had prepared me for this ordeal and because I had seen Him work in my life in countless trials … I knew I could trust Him. God will see us through any trial – great or small.

Can you trust the God who saved you and gave you eternal life to be the God who is with you today?

✝   Marilyn Phillips

29 ✟ ROCK SOLID FOUNDATION

Therefore everyone who hears these words of mine and puts them into practice is like a wise man who built his house on the rock. The rain came down, the streams rose, and the winds blew and beat against that house; yet it did not fall, because it had its foundation on the rock.

Matthew 7:24-25

I was a high school cheerleader coach and went with the team to a Christian Cheerleaders of America Camp each year where they worked on techniques and fundamentals.

Cheerleaders know the importance of a strong base. The person at the base often will hold another girl at arm's length over her head supporting her in a Liberty or Scorpion position. Always, the physically strongest cheerleader is on the bottom of the mount as the base. The motivation is simple: the girl on the top wants a strong foundation. When weak members are on the bottom, the girls will tumble and fall.

Do you have a strong foundation? Christians understand this concept very well. The Rock of our Salvation, Jesus Christ, is all the foundation that is needed. Without a strong base, it is difficult to stand firm as a Christian and avoid the tumbles and falls of life.

Are your feet planted firmly on the rock solid foundation of Jesus Christ?

✟   Marilyn Phillips

FRUIT OF THE SPIRIT

But the fruit of the Spirit is love, joy, peace, patience, kindness, goodness, faithfulness, gentleness and self-control.
Galatians 5:22

30 ✝ THE FRUIT OF THE SPIRIT

But the fruit of the Spirit is love, joy, peace, patience, kindness, goodness, faithfulness, gentleness and self-control. Against such things there is no law. Those who belong to Christ Jesus have crucified the sinful nature with its passions and desires. Since we live by the Spirit, let us keep in step with the Spirit. Let us not become conceited, provoking and envying each other.
Galatians 5:22-26

In these verses, we find a list of the characteristics of the fruit of the Spirit. Note that the word "fruit" is singular. There is just one. The Spirit of God creates this fruit in us. Galatians tells us what this fruit looks like. It has at least nine traits.

These traits can be described as characteristics or actions that come from God alone. So when we look at the trait that we are weakest in, that shows us how mature we are in Christ – we are only as mature as our weakest trait.

In the next nine pages, we will step through each characteristic of the fruit of the Spirit.

Are you allowing God to create His fruit in you?

✝   Rebekah Phillips

31 ☩ LOVE

But the fruit of the Spirit is love …
from Galatians 5:22

The first characteristic of the fruit of the Spirit is love. Our true model of love is Jesus. He laid down his life for us because he loved us so much! Jesus died on the cross for everyone because we are sinners who couldn't pay the price for our sins! Jesus gave us hope and life when He came down to be a man so that we can become more like Him. We can look to Jesus' time on earth to see how He loved others.

All throughout the New Testament, Jesus reminded and encouraged Christians to love. In John 13:34-35, Jesus said, *A new command I give you: Love one another. As I have loved you, so you must love one another. By this all men will know that you are my disciples, if you love one another.*

God wants us to show love to ALL kinds of people, not just to a certain group of people. Love is easy when you get along with other people. Love is harder when you don't get along with others.

One good way to show people that you are a Christian is to love everyone regardless of the situation. If you are a Christian, in what ways are you showing love to others?

How do you show love to the people who are your friends? How can you show love to strangers?

☩   Rebekah Phillips

32 ✟ JOY

But the fruit of the Spirit is … joy …
from Galatians 5:22

Joy is described as having a deep, abiding contentment. This is something that comes from what God has done for us. God saved us from our sin, and wants to have a real relationship with us.

God deemed us special enough to love us, and He knows each person by name! Of course, we will have troubles that can cause discouragement and anger. Having these emotions is normal, but we must remember that we have an all-powerful God. He can do anything through us and overcome every obstacle we face!

I have two diseases, Cystic Fibrosis and CF related diabetes, that frustrate me and can discourage me greatly. When I feel this way, I turn to God to help me have joy. Like all of the traits, joy is a gift of the Spirit. People can tell if you are constantly angry inside or if you have great, abiding joy. Proverbs 27:19 states that, *As water reflects a face, so a man's heart reflects the man.*

What does your face reflect? Whatever is inside your heart will eventually show on your face. Are you secretly upset with a family member or friend? Are you jealous of another's achievement? If yes, please seek God and confess (agree with God that this is wrong) this attitude. Ask Him to show you how to rejoice in their achievement.

What are some ways you can express joy?

✟   Rebekah Phillips

41

33 ✝ PEACE

But the fruit of the Spirit is ... peace ...
from Galatians 5:22

As Christians, we are called to be at peace. Having peace means that God grants us the ability to remain calm in ALL situations.

Our peace must come from God. 1 Corinthians 14:33 reminds us that our God is not a God of disorder but of peace.

When our loved ones are arguing with each other or with us, we don't have to get angry and continue to argue with them. Proverbs 15:1 says, *"A gentle answer turns away wrath, but a harsh word stirs up anger."* God calls us to live above circumstances and trust in our gifts from God.

When nothing is going our way, we don't have to be in a bad mood. We have the ability that comes from God to have peace in any situation.

We can choose to be peaceful so that others can see God in our lives. So, how can you have peace in stressful situations? Claim God's promises in the Bible.

Will you depend on God to bring you peace today?

✝   Rebekah Phillips

34 ✞ PATIENCE

But the fruit of the Spirit is ... patience ...
from Galatians 5:22

Patience is another way to be like Christ. I tend to be impatient. I am impatient when another person takes a loooonnngg time when we work on a project, or when I have to wait in the doctor's office forever. I get upset that they are not moving at my pace.

Recently, I have learned to look to God when I get impatient with others. I don't like it when people get impatient with me. God is forever patient with me. He instructs me to be patient with others. James 5:7 says, *Be patient, then, brothers, until the Lord's coming. See how the farmer waits for the land to yield its valuable crop and how patient he is for the autumn and spring rains.*

When you have patience, you are not rushing through things that could cause you to make mistakes along the way. When I rushed my homework projects in college, I made many mistakes. I had to spend more time to undo my mistakes. When I practiced patience and took my time, I only had to do the project once.

There is much satisfaction in doing things slower and the right way. What things cause you to be impatient? Do others get impatient with you?

Have you asked God to help you with your impatience?

✞   Rebekah Phillips

35 ☦ KINDNESS

But the fruit of the Spirit is ... kindness ...
from Galatians 5:22

Some synonyms for kindness are respectful, grace, favor, mercy, and service. Don't you appreciate when someone says an encouraging word to you? A little kindness can go a long way.

Kindness can brighten someone's day. John 4:1-26 tells the story of Jesus being kind to the Samaritan woman. Because Jesus was kind to this woman, He was able to witness to her, and the woman became a follower of Christ. Without Jesus being kind, this woman may not have believed that He was sent from God.

In a fast pace society, do we take the time to show kindness to all sorts of people?

Do we give grace to those who cut us off or shove us to the side with their actions?

How often do we serve others on a daily basis?

How can your kind actions change someone's day or life?

☦   Rebekah Phillips

36 ☦ GOODNESS

But the fruit of the Spirit is … goodness …

from Galatians 5:22

Goodness is another characteristic of the fruit of the Spirit. Some synonyms of goodness are decency, honesty, and rightness.

Being good can be a hard thing, but we need to be good so that people can see a difference in our lives as we walk with God. If we don't portray the characteristics of Christ, we are not letting God shine through our lives, and we are not being positive witnesses for Christ.

We must pray for God to show His goodness through us. We are called to be good wherever we are – at work, at church, at home, or out with friends. Also, we can ask ourselves some questions to see if our actions or choices reflect the goodness of Christ. Is what I say or wear appropriate? Am I being honest? Am I showing love to others? Anyone can be honest and tell the truth in a kind manner without hurting another person's feelings.

How often do I tell the truth to others? Are my actions honorable before God?

☦   Rebekah Phillips

37 ✞ FAITHFULNESS

But the fruit of the Spirit is ... faithfulness ...

from Galatians 5:22

Faith is one of the main traits we should have as Christians! Without faith, we can't believe in Christ. With faith in Christ, anything is possible! As Jesus said in Matthew 17:20b, *I tell you the truth, if you have faith as small as mustard seed, you can say to this mountain, 'Move from here to there' and it will move. Nothing will be impossible for you.*

Also, God wants us to have a childlike faith as written in Matthew 19:13-14. These verses state, *Then little children were brought to Jesus for him to place his hands on them and pray for them. But the disciples rebuked those who brought them. Jesus said, "Let the little children come to me, and do not hinder them, for the kingdom of heaven belongs to such as these."*

I am a preschool teacher in a Christian environment. Whenever I teach about God, the children are so excited, and they are awed by Jesus' miracles. I think God wants us to continue being excited and awed by what He did for us, what He is doing for us, and what He will do for us in the future!

Have you lost your excitement for God? What can you do to rediscover your excitement about God? Can you focus on God's faithfulness?

✞   Rebekah Phillips

38 ✞ GENTLENESS

But the fruit of the Spirit is ... gentleness ...
from Galatians 5:22-23

Gentleness can be described as being considerate. This is so hard for me to do sometimes. I have to admit I tend to think about my needs before others.

I confess that sometimes I am just not considerate toward others. I expect the other person to meet my need instead of me meeting the other person's need. This is wrong and leads to much discord! If every Christian meets another's need, then everyone's need will be met. This is the way the early church served each other as shown in Acts.

The definition for gentleness includes not being harsh. This caused me to think about the many times I have been harsh in my own life. Sometimes I was harsh on material things like slamming doors out of anger – but it wasn't the thing that made me angry, it was another person. Sometimes what I said was harsh and hurt another person's feelings. I never felt good about it later.

Do you have temper tantrums when things don't go your way or your needs aren't met? What are the ways you can be gentle with both your things and other people?

✞   Rebekah Phillips

39 ✞ SELF-CONTROL

But the fruit of the Spirit is ... self-control ...
from Galatians 5:22-23

Self-control is the last characteristic of the fruit of the Spirit mentioned in Scripture. This has always been the hardest for me.

Growing up, sometimes I had trouble focusing on my homework. Often, I waited until the last minute to do a school project and didn't do a good job because I hurried through it. Over time, I learned to use self-control and write down what I needed to do in order and work my way down the list.

I also find it hard to control my emotions or anger in an argument and I end up saying things I regret. Sometimes I just need to stop a disagreement to cool down. When I take the time to control my anger, I can be more sensible and find a solution that works for all people involved.

In the Bible, there are many verses that encourage us to have self-control. James 1:20 says to control our anger *for man's anger does not bring about the righteous life that God desires*, and James 3:1-12 says to watch what you say.

What are the areas of self-control where you need to focus?

✞   Rebekah Phillips

GOD'S PLANS

"For I know the plans I have for you," declares the LORD, "plans to prosper you and not to harm you, plans to give you hope and a future."
Jeremiah 29:11

40 ✞ GOD'S ARMOR

Put on the full armor of God so that you can take your stand against the devil's schemes. For our struggle is not against flesh and blood, but against the rulers, against the authorities, against the powers of this dark world and against the spiritual forces of evil in the heavenly realms.
Ephesians 6:11-12

We are in a great cosmic, spiritual battle between good and evil. Most of the people around us are totally unaware of it. God gives Christians the discernment to see what is happening. Review the armor God provided. It is listed in Ephesians 6. Don't go into battle without all of your armor.

We need to "suit up" each morning by putting on our armor of God just like a football player puts on pads and a helmet before a game. This will equip us for battles of the day. We need to be prepared and equipped.

Teachers don't approach a classroom unprepared. I was a second grade teacher for over eighteen years and it took great planning to be equipped to teach each day. Christians shouldn't approach life without the same attention to their daily preparations.

Do you realize that God has prepared you for every life battle that you will encounter? Are you using God's armor?

✞   Marilyn Phillips

41 ✞ DRESS FOR THE BATTLE

If I'm the light of the world,
No wonder things seem so dark.
My shield of faith has a big crack,
Scared cries tumble from my heart.

Father, I need to climb into Your arms,
And soak up Your loving thoughts.
"Come unto Me, Child", You kindly say,
"My Son has covered all of your faults.

It's a dark and dangerous world,
You tried to fight the battles alone.
Soldiers who fight without the right clothes,
Are sure to stumble on every stone.

Put on this garment of love,
And My belt of truth.
Protect your heart with My righteousness,
Stand firm in these peaceful shoes.

Focus on Me and your faith will be,
Stronger than any shield you've seen.
Pick up the sword of My Word,
My saving helmet will guard what you think.

It's a dark and dangerous world,
You tried to fight the battles alone.
Soldiers who fight without the right clothes,
Are sure to stumble on every stone.

You don't have to shine all alone,
The cares of this world are like a fog.
Shake them off and you'll shine like a star,
Reflect My light from deep in your heart.

When you fall you can get right back up,
The pain from your falls and trials.
Give humility and compassion,
And make you more like My Child.

It's a dark and dangerous world,
You tried to fight the battles alone.
Soldiers who fight without the right clothes,
Are sure to stumble on every stone.

Sliding down from Your Mighty Arms,
Testing the ground on these shoes of Peace.
Looking around from the glow of Your presence,
Things couldn't get much brighter than this.

My shield of faith is stronger than ever,
Sure to deflect each fiery dart.
Praising You, Father, You are mighty,
Reflecting the light You put in my heart.

Though it's a dark and dangerous world,
I know the war has already been won.
Soldiers prepared for the battles,
Glow in victory through Your Precious Son.

✝   ©Tamara Roberts

42 ✝ GOD'S HELMET AND SWORD

Take the helmet of salvation and the sword of the Spirit, which is the word of God.
Ephesians 6:17

A football helmet can help protect the player from injury. But, it can only help if the player actually puts the helmit on and wears it. Christians have our relationship with God as our helmet, but like the helmet we have to put it on. Just knowing a lot about the helmet, or God, doesn't protect. You must use it!

The world is always trying to penetrate our minds with many ungodly messages. Our faith is what deflects negative messages just as a football helmet protects the player's head. God also gave us a sword – His Word. This is our weapon both for offense and defense.

Do you memorized God's Words so Bible verses are in your heart? Just like Jesus, we must fall back on the Word when tempted.

Have you put on the helmet of salvation?

Are you trusting the Word of God as your sword of protection for today?

✝   Marilyn Phillips

43 ✞ LEADERSHIP

She is clothed with strength and dignity; she can laugh at the days to come. She speaks with wisdom, and faithful instruction is on her tongue. She watches over the affairs of her household and does not eat the bread of idleness. Her children arise and call her blessed; her husband also, and he praises her: "Many women do noble things, but you surpass them all."
Proverbs 31:25-29

A good leader has quality characteristics. A good leader respects herself and is happy. She gets her wisdom from God and is very knowledgeable whenever she speaks. A good leader is faithful to God. She works hard. The people she leads think very highly of her. Proverbs 29:2 states: W*hen the righteous thrive, the people rejoice; when the wicked rule, the people groan*, and Proverbs 29:4 says: *By justice a king gives a country stability, but one who is greedy for bribes tears it down.*

Haven't you seen these leadership qualities to be true in our nation? We prosper under Godly leaders but do not prosper under others.

These verses in Proverbs remind me that a good leader brings joy and stability and a bad leader brings misery and tears down everything. What does a bad leader do in a work setting? What effect does a bad leader bring?

Have you seen what a good leader does and the effects of a good leader? What kind of leader are you?

✞　　　Marilyn Phillips

44 ✟ COMFORT

Praise is to the God and Father of our Lord Jesus Christ, the Father of compassion and the God of all comfort, who comforts us in all our troubles, so that we can comfort those in any trouble with the comfort we ourselves have received from God.
2 Corinthian 1:3-4

When my wonderful dad, Lloyd White, passed away, I was grief stricken. I knew that he was a Christian and going to Heaven, but I missed him so very much. I missed talking with my dad and hearing his kind voice.

My Christian friends brought food for the family, sent cards and e-mails. I knew they were praying for my family during this time of grief and it helped ease the sorrow. God let me experience the power of their ministry to my aching heart. Now, I know better how to comfort others going through similar situations.

Have you ever been comforted in your time of troubles? Sometimes it is a big thing like my dad's death; sometimes it is a small life issue or a personal crisis that you are facing. Here is the point: we all need the comfort of the Father and comfort from our Christian friends.

Whom can you comfort today?

✟   Marilyn Phillips

45 ✞ GOD HAS PLANS FOR ME

"For I know the plans I have for you," declares the LORD, "plans to prosper you and not to harm you, plans to give you hope and a future."
Jeremiah 29:11

During difficult times, we often think that God is punishing us or that we are simply forgotten. But, that's just not true!

God promises that His plans are to prosper you and give you hope. Does that mean that everyone will be wealthy and live a life without sickness or trials? Of course not! It means that God has plans for you beyond anything that can be imagined.

God's plans are to give you hope and a future. Here's a question: If you trusted God with your eternal destination of Heaven, can you trust Him to guide you through the trials of today? Jesus said He is the same yesterday, today and forever (see Hebrews 13:8) – you can depend on Him in the future because you can see His actions in the past.

Do you trust God with your future?

✞   Marilyn Phillips

46 ✟ WHAT WILL I DO?

How exciting, a trip to Lubbock in my first car!
It's only 100 miles – not very far.

Only God knew the event to take place,
Soon angels would be dispatched to act out God's grace.

Right in front of us a car has rolled in our lane,
They weren't watching – the only way to explain.

We moved to the next lane to miss the car,
They moved in our lane, this is bizarre!

I brace for the crash, he turns the car for a broadside impact,
There's only a split second, no time to react.

I must have passed out before the collision,
We were thrown out on the road, not something I would
envision.

Don't move her, her neck could be broken,
Am I dreaming, or did I hear these words spoken.

The lady placed her satin-lined coat over my face,
It's as if I'm in another time and another place.

Is this it, God, will I be with you today?
This would be a good time to pray.

My relationship with God wasn't there yet,
But His angels had been dispatched, don't forget.

In and out of consciousness;
the noisy siren blares

The ambulance races to the hospital,
I'm convinced there were prayers.

All of a sudden, the smelling salts take effect,
I'm free to go, I've been checked.

When I look back on that day long ago,
I realize God's love and grace were at full flow.

"God saved you for a purpose," my grandmother said,
"You could have just as easily been dead."

Yes, in the blink of an eye, I could have died,
But God's protection was provided.

Why me, oh God, why have you spared me?
What is my purpose - this I plea.

What is your purpose? Has God shown you?
Have you asked Him, "What will I do?"

✝   ©Beth Peery

47 ✞ TRUST

You intended to harm me, but God intended it for good to accomplish what is now being done, the saving of many lives.

Genesis 50:20

Joseph's brothers sold him into slavery. Once their father Jacob died, they were afraid that Joseph would take revenge on them. However, Joseph had matured in the Lord to where he saw through circumstances that God's hand was on his life. This is the Old Testament equivalent of Romans 8:28, *"And we know that in all things God works for the good of those who love him, who have been called according to his purpose."*

When things seem to be against you, and you know you have done nothing wrong, it is time to learn to trust in the Lord!

Do you see God at work through your frustrations? Maybe you don't, but God promises that He is there working things out for good just like He did in Joseph's time.

Start looking for the promises He gives you in the Bible.

Will you trust God in difficult situations?

✞   Marilyn Phillips

48 ✞ TRUSTING GOD'S PLANS

No eye has seen, no ear has heard, no mind has conceived what God has prepared for those who love him.

1 Corinthians 2:9

We can't even conceive the plans that God has for us. If we pray and read the Bible, God will reveal his plans. One summer, I went to the doctor for a mammogram. The results indicated breast cancer. I was shocked and wondered how this could be God's plan for me!

Through this cancer journey I have seen a BIGGER GOD. I had surgery to remove the tumor and six weeks of radiation. Now, I have a new awareness of God's presence in my life! I realized that God is greater than anything and any battle that I will ever encounter. I have a new boldness to share my faith with others. This cancer battle changed my perspective. God has prepared for me a ministry to others with cancer.

Are you aware of how much God loves you? When in a difficult situation, do you ask "Why me?" Or, do you immediately depend on God? The real question to ask God is, "What now?"

God uses both the bad things and the good things in life to reveal His presence to you.

What does God have prepared for you today?

✞   Marilyn Phillips

49 ✝ WORK HARD

She selects wool and flax and works with eager hands. She is like the merchant ships, bringing her food from afar. She gets up while it is still dark; she provides food for her family and portions for her servant girls. She considers a field and buys it; out of her earnings she plants a vineyard. She sets about her work vigorously; her arms are strong for her tasks.

Proverbs 31:13-17

A good leader is a hard worker and plans ahead. She sets goals and gets things done. A leader understands that work can last all day but she knows that diligence can pay off for her team in the workplace or at church. Work can build character.

After working hard on a project, I feel like I have accomplished something great. Do you do your best at all times? In what areas do you need to work harder?

I have discovered that when I work hard at doing things that I will honor God. *"Whatever you do, work at it with all your heart, as working for the Lord, not for men."* Colossians 3:23

Are you setting goals so the work God has for you will be accomplished?

✝   Rebekah Phillips

GOD'S DIRECTIONS

Direct me in the path of your commands, for there I find delight.

Psalms 119:35

50 ✝ ACTIONS PORTRAY YOUR FAITH

What good is it, my brothers, if a man claims to have faith but has no deeds? Can such faith save him? Suppose a brother or sister is without clothes and daily food. If one of you says to him, "Go, I wish you well; keep warm and well fed," but does nothing about his physical needs, what good is it? In the same way, faith by itself, if it is not accompanied by action, is dead.

James 2:14-17

Have you noticed some friends say one thing, but do something else instead? For example, have you ever seen someone say that they will not gossip, but you turn around and hear them share negative comments about a friend?

This is how some Christians act. People say that they are Christians but they never do godly things. Pay attention to 1 Timothy 4:16 which says to *Watch your life and doctrine closely. Persevere in them, because if you do, you will save both yourself and your hearers*. This encourages Christians to reflect God at ALL times in our public and private actions.

Do your actions reflect your knowledge of God? When you are around people, does what you say and do reflect God?

When you are alone in your room, do your thoughts and actions reflect God?

Does your walk match your talk?

✝   Marilyn Phillips

51 ✞ HOW ARE WE TO DO THIS FAITH?

Trust in God, what does that mean?
Are we to have faith in the One not seen?
Are we to give our life to the One who was sent?
By confessing our sin, and then repent?

Are we to turn away from sin by which we are entangled,
The sin that makes us feel like we're being strangled?
Are we to surrender and say, "I can't do it without You, Lord,"
And make sure our commitment is never ignored?

Are we to pray to God at all times without ceasing,
And feel sin's hold ever decreasing?
Are we to seek God's plan for our life on earth,
The one He knew before our birth?

Are we to read the Bible and listen quietly,
For the leading that comes ever so gently?
Are we to put our faith in action,
Regardless of friends' reaction?

Are we to love all whether enemies or friends,
With a love no one comprehends?
Are we to always live strong and persevere,
For we know our Lord will soon be here?

YOU know in your heart these things you must do,
"Follow Me," Jesus has whispered to you.

✞   ©Beth Peery

52 ✟ STUMBLING BLOCK

Accept him whose faith is weak, without passing judgment on disputable matter. Therefore let us stop passing judgment on one another. Instead, make up your mind not to put any stumbling block or obstacle in your brother's way.
Romans 14:1, 13

There were many times I shared my faith with others and people refused to believe that Christianity is the only way. They either didn't believe in any God or thought that all religions should be considered equal.

It was hard for me to accept the way that some people are thinking. I know without a doubt that there is only one way to God and that many are closing their minds to that one way, Jesus Christ. I can only pray for them and show them respect even though we disagree.

God convicted me that if I don't show them respect, don't listen to why they believe what they do, or if I judge them, then I have lost any future opportunities to witness to them and to show them God's love. Arguing will only cause others to stumble. Without the opportunity to hear God's Word, they will never believe. I encourage you to pray for the people who believe differently from you so you will know how to share God's Word and love for them!

Is there someone in your life that you have caused to stumble through your actions or words? If the answer is yes, what should you do?

✟   Rebekah Phillips

53 ✞ GOD IS OUR REFUGE AND STRENGTH

God is our refuge and strength, an ever-present help in trouble.

Psalm 46:1

There is really not a picture that you can view that does Andrews' Glacier justice. It looks like an ordinary glacier that people could slide down very easily. I remember over thirty years ago that we took a hike to the bottom of the glacier. From that view, it did not look difficult to go down from the top.

In 2013, on our family vacation to Colorado, it was decided that we would slid down the glacier. Hum ... I was thinking ... should I do this? Being over sixty, I wondered if I could make it, but, I decided I would go anyway. There were six of us that took the hike, including three of our grandchildren.

The morning came to "make the slide." My son-in-law asked me to pray for our protection and safety. We wanted to be "covered in prayer." God knew what was ahead, and He was with us.

As we got to the glacier, the site was unbelievable. It was three times as big as I thought it would be and I could see people sliding on ice, hugging their poles and walking (inching) very carefully. Our son-in-law went ahead of us and tested the terrain and said it was okay to join him. Every step that I took, I slid, even with great hiking boots. I walked sideways, laid on my back and slid, used my hiking poles, and slid down part of the way tandem. Now I knew why we prayed for God's safety and protection.

My husband, Keith, went to help with two of our granddaughters. As I tried to move forward, I would start sliding and couldn't stop. As I lay flat on the ice after falling, a young man, seventeen years old, asked me if he could help me get down to the rocks. I said, "Yes!" As he walked in front to lead the way, I was still sliding. So, he took my hand with his warm, gloved hand and carefully started walking me down the glacier to the rocks below and safety.

I was reminded of my prayer. I had probably made a big mistake sliding down that glacier but God was with me. I told the young man that I had prayed that morning for our protection, and I that I believed that God had sent him, like an angel, to help me down to the rocks. He said that he didn't feel God was using him. I asked him if he believed in God and prayer and he said yes. And I said I knew God had used him to keep me from falling and to keep me safe. I felt like one of the reasons I was there was to encourage a young man who did not think God could use him to help.

I was able to share with the young man's family how I believed God had sent their son to help me. Isn't it amazing how God had that family there while our family was there?

I thank God for His protection for me and my family. I thank God that He sends people to help us no matter where we are. I am grateful that God listens to our prayers and answers them. He is my help in my ever present time of need, even when I put myself in "harm's way." Thank you, Lord for rescuing me every day!!!

Do you believe that God will protect you in your time of need?

☦   Donna Kirkendoll

54 ✞ CAREFUL WORDS

Do not let any unwholesome talk come out of your mouths, but only what is helpful for building others up according to their needs, that it may benefit those who listen. Be kind and compassionate to one another, forgiving each other, just as in Christ God forgave you.
Ephesians 4:29,32

You have heard the saying, "Sticks and stones may break my bones, but words will never hurt me." This just isn't true – it is wishful thinking. Words can be VERY hurtful!!! Mean words are very hard to forget. You can NEVER take back the hurtful things you say.

Kind words can make your spirit soar and uplifts others. Calming words can help stop someone from being stressed or angry. I encourage you to consider what you say to anyone that crosses your path and especially the words that you say to your friends.

Do your words hurt other people's feelings or encourage them? Is the tone of your voice bitter and angry? Are you tearing down someone to others? How kind are you to others? Do you quickly forgive?

Are you careful with words?

✞   Marilyn Phillips

55 ✝ BE WISE

Be very careful, then, how you live - not as unwise but as wise, making the most of every opportunity, because the days are evil. Therefore do not be foolish, but understand what the Lord's will is.
Ephesians 5:15-17

Let's face it, every day we hear about all the evil events happening in the news. As time goes on, the world will have more evil. When I was growing up, I remember my teachers, my parents, and my parents' friends saying that they could not believe how evil the world is getting or that things were not this bad when they were growing up. I groaned every time they said this, but now I am an adult, and I am saying the exact same thing that they did. Things HAVE gotten worse in my lifetime. You probably are saying the same thing to your children.

In Revelations, there are prophecies that say times will continue to worsen until the second coming of Christ. The only way Christians can be wise is to study the Bible. I love reading the book of Proverbs because this book helps to define a wise man and a foolish man. The wise will witness (tell what they have seen and experienced) to others. The days are evil and we need to reach everybody that we can.

Are you making the most of every opportunity to make wise choices by understanding God's will for you?

✝   Rebekah Phillips

56 ✝ THE BIBLE MATTERS

Direct me in the path of your commands, for there I find delight.
Psalms 119:35

Psalms 119 is the longest chapter in the Bible. It teaches us why the Bible matters. Dr. Scott Maze says, "The Bible has sin-killing power, but it also has mind-blowing beauty!"

Hebrews calls the Word of God a two-edged sword that can test our motives and emotions. Not only that, the Word challenges areas of our lives that are not pleasing to God. *Is not my word like fire,"* declares the LORD, *"and like a hammer that breaks a rock in pieces?"* (Jeremiah 23:29)

The Word describes itself as a fire that burns inside believers! This fiery truth wants to get out and warm those around us. His holy hammer breaks down our motives and reveals our hearts' intent. For these statements to be true in our lives, we must experience the Bible, not just simply read it. Jesus said He sent the Holy Spirit to live in us that we might know Him in a real and personal way.

When we are still before God in prayer and meditation, the Spirit confirms His Word in us and it becomes real to us. Do you make time to delight in the Word of God? The Bible matters!

Do you let God build His character in you through daily intake of His Word?

✝ Marilyn Phillips

57 ✞ DO NOT BE DECEIVED

Let no one deceive you with empty words, for because of such things God's wrath comes on those who are disobedient. Therefore do not be partners with them. For you were once darkness, but now you are light in the Lord. Live as children of light.

Ephesians 5:6-8

We see so many advertisements that promise us something but can't fulfill that promise. There are so many unfulfilled promises from billboards, books, magazines, newspapers, news stations, radio and the internet. We are promised that if we use this shampoo, our hair will look beautiful and we will get more dates; if you drink this soda, you are fun; if you use a certain toothpaste, your teeth will be sparkling white and everyone will notice you.

I have tried using the shampoo, soda, and toothpaste, but I didn't get results that the commercials promised. I am tempted to listen to what the world promises through the false ads, but I can't let myself be deceived.

The only way to avoid deception is by studying and reading what the Bible says. Praying helps me not to be deceived. God always reveals the truth to me.

Where do you find truth?

✞   Rebekah Phillips

58 ✝ WELLSPRING OF LIFE

Above all else, guard your heart, for it is the wellspring of life.
Proverbs 4:23

The Bible tells us in several places to guard our hearts, and to be careful of the things that we read, see or hear. What goes in your mind will eventually come out through your words and actions! *The good man brings good things out of the good stored up in him, and the evil man brings evil things out of the evil stored up in him* (Matthew 12:35). So, think about how you spend your spare time.

On your way home from work, what type of music do you listen to. Much of today's secular music has angry words. Could you choose instead to listen to Christian music with uplifting words? Think about the books that you are reading. Are the books worthy of your time? When you go to a theater, do you carefully select the movies that you watch?

The Bible challenges us to guard our hearts? So, how can you guard your heart? Do you evaluate books, movies or music at their core level? Try to formulate in one sentence what the message of each song, book or movie is.

Is it something you would be proud to share with Jesus?

What are you doing to guard your heart today? Do you have a wellspring or source of continual supply for your life?

✝   Marilyn Phillips

GOD'S PROVISIONS

Be joyful always; pray continually; give thanks in all circumstances, for this is God's will for you in Christ Jesus.

1 Thessalonians 5:16-18

59 ✞ POWER OF PRAYER

Again, I tell you that if two of you on earth agree about anything you ask for, it will be done for you by my Father in heaven. For where two or three come together in my name, there am I with them.
Matthew 18:19-20

Some time ago, I thought I was only going for a regular checkup for Cystic Fibrosis. I regularly do pulmonary function tests (PFTs). These tests measure the lung's capacity to take in and exhale air. This day, my lung functions were in the thirty percentile range which is dangerously low. One of the doctors introduced the possibility of having a double lung transplant in the future if my lung functions continued at less than thirty percent.

My PFTs have remained in the thirty percent range for ten years. The power of united prayer from our friends and family has worked. Our prayer chain extends from coast to coast and even halfway around the world to friends in India.

The CF doctor is amazed with my activity level despite my low lung functions. I graduated from college in 2002. Since then, I have worked as a part-time teacher. I exercise and swim daily, and stay active in my church. Recently, I even won a contest at my gym. Each hour of exercise class participation at the gym was recorded and I won the contest with a total of seventy-eight hours of exercise in one month. Normally, a person with low lung functions is in declining health and needs oxygen and requires many hospital stays.

Do you believe in the power of united prayer?

✞   Rebekah Phillips

60 ✝ PRAYER

Prayer is the privilege of talking to God in Heaven,
We have the opportunity to speak with Him twenty-four seven.
Our Lord is on call all the time,
That means not just mealtime or bedtime.

You ask, "Why should we pray if He knows what we think?
Just to hear ourselves talk, you say with a wink?"
Prayer is not something to take lightly,
You are speaking with the Lord God Almighty.

It's not a time to ask for favors,
Or tell Him how much you dislike the neighbors.
It's a time to praise and worship our Lord,
To confess and ask for forgiveness of any discord.

Tell Him how grateful and thankful you've been;
After all, everything you are and have comes from Him.
There are burdens on your heart for family and friends;
This is when you ask our Lord to make amends.

He's your Heavenly Father and He loves you so,
He wants your relationship to grow.
Everyone sins, but God doesn't see,
Because Jesus' blood covers us, making us free.

Free from what you say?
Free from sins' barrier so you can pray.

✝   ©Beth Peery

61 ✞ TALKING TO GOD

Be joyful in hope, patient in affliction, faithful in prayer.
Romans 12:12

The word "hope" in the New Testament means "confident assurance." Substitute that phrase for "hope" each time you see it in the Bible. We are to be joyful, or rejoice, because we have a confident assurance.

Look at the context of this verse in Romans 12. Paul is telling us how to live – how to *offer your bodies as living sacrifices, holy and pleasing to God - this is your spiritual act of worship.* Then he says to be *patient in affliction.* "Patient" means to persevere or "hang tight," or to endure or carry bravely and calmly. The word "Affliction" can mean tribulation or stress – it carries the idea of being "pressed."

So when our situation presses us, we are to endure bravely and calmly. How? We know in our hearts that Jesus led the way. Finally, the verse tells us to be *faithful in prayer.* The Greek word can also mean "devoted" and carries the idea of "adhering." Prayer is just talking to God, so this part of the verse could be interpreted as saying, "Glue yourself to your conversations with God!" Do you rejoice because you are confident in Christ? Do you "bear up" under pressure? Do you pray only when you are facing a difficult situation?

Praying is talking to God. Have you been faithful in prayer today?

✞   Marilyn Phillips

62 ✝ NOT ALONE ON THIS JOURNEY

Carry each other's burdens, and in this way you will fulfill the law of Christ.
Galatians 6:2

Family and friends rejoiced with us when our first grandson was born. To add to the excitement, my husband received a wonderful gift when Caleb arrived on his forty-eighth birthday.

The first eighteen months of Caleb's life were typical. He grew into a happy, interactive toddler. My grandson would run to me with his little outstretched arms squealing, "Grammy!" He was learning to talk and could correctly point to and say about a dozen words in addition to parent/grandparent names. Then suddenly ... things started to change!

Caleb stopped talking within three months. This little boy was no longer interactive with anyone. The only thing my grandson would do with his toys by this time was to line them up on the floor. And that's the way they had to stay. If any toys got moved my grandson would scream for hours and writhe in what appeared to be pain. Eye contact with Caleb ceased to exist and he could not be touched or the screaming and wild flailing would begin again.

Even before a doctor made it official, just before Caleb's second birthday, we all knew there was a serious problem. It was Autism.

We were all heartbroken. I feared for my precious grandson. What kind of a future could he have? Would he ever be a happy little boy again? Would this child be able to go to school with autism?

Would Caleb ever be independent? I was afraid the strain on his parents' marriage might be overwhelming. Soon I realized my fears were the same as Caleb's parents and his other grandparents. This was just too much for us to bear alone.

Thankfully we were not alone. We took our concerns to God. We learned to give all our concerns to Him.   God directed our paths.

We needed support from each other and from our extended family and friends. Through e-mail we kept everyone informed. Family and friends always knew how to pray for our grandson and his family. Through those prayers, challenging financial, physical, and emotional needs were met. Caleb's parents said they could sense the prayers being lifted up for them. Even though the future was unsure for our grandson, we all had the assurance God was with us on this journey.

Who needs your help with a burden or life journey?

✞   Anita Barngrover

63 ✞ UNITE IN PRAYER

Therefore confess your sins to each other and pray for each other so that you may be healed. The prayer of a righteous man is powerful and effective.

James 5:16

I am a member of a large Sunday School class where we pray specifically for needs of those who are present that day. It is so comforting to hear a room full of people lift up your prayer needs to God. Not only that, but God promises us power when we agree together in prayer.

I'm also part of a group of ladies who meet for lunch each Wednesday. We call ourselves the "Lunch Bunch" and we read Scripture and share prayer requests and praises. We have experienced answers to prayers that are beyond all expectations. Are you part of a group that prays regularly?

We have learned that when sharing prayer requests in groups it is best to follow a few guidelines.

- Share the essence of the request, not all of the details. (Keep those details to yourself.)
- Respect privacy – do not let prayer requests become the subject of gossip.
- Don't monopolize the group – let everyone have an opportunity to share.
- Sincerely seek the will of God on all matters.

Do you make time with your Sunday School group or Bible Study group to pray each time you are together?

✞   Marilyn Phillips

64 ✟ WHAT HAPPENS WHEN FRIENDS PRAY?

What happens when friends pray?
Let me tell you … they stay with you all the way!
Through the hard days, through the sad days,
Through the up and down days, Through the gray days,
They stay with you all the way!

On their knees they go,
Every time you need them so.
Petitioning to our Lord and Savior,
There will never be a failure.
For they know how powerful prayer can be,
Just try it and you will see!

God says where two or more of My children will be,
You just have to ask and all agree.
There I am thus saith the Lord,
Your petitions will not be ignored.
He hears all the prayers,
And I know that He cares.

My friends have prayed for me,
And also for my family.
They prayed for the sadness to go away,
So that peace and memories would find a way.
We feel the prayers, it's easier each day,
To see the light instead of the gray.

Thank you dear friends, what would we do without you?
We need each other to help us get through.
To God be the glory, the great healer is He,
But He still works through you and me!

✟   ©Beth Peery

65 ✞ MEMORIZE SCRIPTURE

I have hidden your word in my heart that I might not sin against you.
Psalms 119:11

When we hide something, we have put it somewhere for safe keeping and we know where to find It when needed. The Bible verses that we memorize are tucked away in our hearts. We hide them away in our minds like a treasure. When we meditate on Scripture, it is like taking our treasure out of hiding and admiring it over and over.

We can understand God's commands better when we have memorized them. How can we identify a sin against God if we don't read and memorize the Scriptures? When we fill up our minds with Scripture, we can easily carry it with us and access it whenever we need it. This verse in Psalms 119 promises that when we know Scripture it will work to prevent sin in our life.

I have found that God brings the perfect Scripture to my mind at just the right time. Have you hidden Scripture in your heart?

Do you have a plan for regularly memorizing Scripture? Who holds you accountable for memorizing Scripture? Could you and a friend memorize Scripture together? How about memorizing one Scripture per week ?

✞   Marilyn Phillips

66 ✝ MEDITATION

Let me understand the teaching of your precepts;
then I will meditate on your wonders.
Psalms 119:27

Meditation is when we reflect deeply on a subject. It helps to be in a quiet place. A good place to meditate on Scripture would be in your room or outside on the patio. Meditation requires us to think over Scripture while seeking what insights God's Spirit may provide.

There are many ways to approach meditation, so let's look at some practical suggestions.

- Memorize a Scripture verse, or verses.
- Go over it in your mind one word at a time thinking about what each word means.
- If there are pronouns, substitute I, me, mine, etc., for the more general pronouns.
- You can even put your own name in place of those pronouns. The goal is to see yourself in the Bible verse.
- Visualize what the verse is describing. Are there sounds? Are there smells? Was it warm or cold?

Try to put yourself in that place so you can experience the reality of the verse. When we meditate on Scripture, we focus on the great and mighty God who intervenes in our lives daily.

Have you made time to meditate on the wonders of God?

✝   Marilyn Phillips

67 ✝ GOD WILL RENEW YOU

Even youths grow tired and weary, and young men stumble and fall; but those who hope in the LORD will renew their strength. They will soar on wings like eagles; they will run and not grow weary, they will walk and not be faint.
Isaiah 40:30-31

Weary! Often, the fatigue is so great that it seems we can't take another step. The physical demands of life are overwhelming at times. Maybe that's when you should evaluate the meetings, clubs, and extra-curricular activities that you participate in on a regular basis. Are they all really necessary? Have activities and commitments pushed your quiet time with God out of your life?

Sometimes, others think you should be involved in a ministry that they are involved in ... but, have you prayed about this decision? It might not even be what God wants you to do. It could actually prevent you from doing God's will for you.

It is impossible to be part of all activities at work and at church. Are there any groups or activities that you can eliminate? If you are too busy to have a daily quiet time with God ... you are too busy!

Can you rearrange your schedule so you can get plenty of rest? Take time to eat healthy foods – don't always choose fast food.

God promises to renew your strength. Will you claim that promise?

✝   Marilyn Phillips

68 ✟ DEALING WITH TOUGH TIMES

Be joyful always; pray continually; give thanks in all circumstances, for this is God's will for you in Christ Jesus.
1 Thessalonians 5:16-18

Can you really be joyful always? How can I be joyful if I am not happy about what is happening to me? "Happy" is an emotion. It comes and goes with how we feel or with what we have experienced. "Joy" is a mindset. It is a choice. It is not determined by how we feel or by our situation. Jesus *endured the cross for the joy that was set before Him* (Hebrews 12:2b).

Was Jesus "happy" about what happened on the cross? Do we let the circumstances of life determine our happiness? Can we be joyful in a difficult situation even if we aren't happy with the events?

The key is to be continuously in the presence of God, talking to Him about our experiences, and giving thanks to God no matter the circumstance.

Others are watching us as we witness to them and share our faith in God. Have you given thanks for the situation that you are in today?

Can you be joyful in a difficult situation knowing that God is in control?

✟   Marilyn Phillips

69 ✞ A CHANGED LIFE

No eye has seen, no ear has heard, no mind has conceived what God has prepared for those who love him.

I Corinthians 2:9

"The waiting list is about two or three years for our Adopt-a-Family Program. But go ahead and apply." My heart sank. These were the words I heard over twenty years ago when I first met some people from CAN (Cornerstone Assistance Network). I was a newly single mother of three children ages two, three and four.

I had moved to the Ft. Worth area on faith after much prayer. I knew God had led me to Ft. Worth and knew the timing was right. But, I only had $50 in my pocket. I was frightened about an unknown future. I had thought that the kids and I were going to stay in a pop-up trailer in someone's driveway; but God surprised me and opened the door for us to stay in their home at the very last minute. During the six-week period in these kind people's home, God led me through a series of circumstances to North Richland Hills Baptist Church (NRHBC) and to CAN. It was through this ministry that I learned about Adopt-A-Family. However, when I was told the waiting list was about two or three years, I felt overwhelmed and wondered how I could even provide for my family.

Where could I find a job? While I had three years of college behind me, I had started a family and didn't complete my degree, so I had no marketable skills. God surprised me again when I was hired at a job in a doctor's office that someone from NRHBC helped me find. It was through this contact that God showed me that nursing was what I was to pursue for my career.

In the meantime, I applied for Adopt-A-Family amidst a very difficult separation and divorce (both financially and emotionally) from my children's father. I felt I was falling apart. I was a brand-new Christian and didn't know what was expected of me or what the definition of "Godly" even meant. Somehow, what normally would be years of waiting to be accepted into the program, only took seven days from the date of application to the date of move in. I believe that was the act of certain people and the Hand of God.

The people from both NRHBC and CAN not only provided for my family, but showed me and my children love over and over. I had never seen or felt that kind of unconditional love and acceptance before. It touched me and changed me ... forever.

Because of this ministry, I was able to complete nursing school and obtain my RN. I later obtained a Nursing Case Manager Certification. I now have a career; yes, the very one God had many years earlier shown me about. God took a woman who was searching for a better life for her children to a woman with a college degree and an amazing career.

I learned that God is indeed faithful. He uses many incredible, kind, and loving people to touch lives. My now-grown children and I are just some examples of this.   Words ... well, they are just not adequate this side of Heaven to express not only our gratitude, but how our lives have been impacted because of CAN and a God who provides beyond anything I could have imagined.

Do you believe that God has plans for your life?

✝   Donna DuFrane

70 ✟ WHAT DO YOU TREASURE?

Do not store up for yourselves treasures on earth, where moth and rust destroy, and where thieves break in and steal. But store up for yourselves treasures in heaven, where moth and rust do not destroy, and where thieves do not break in and steal. For where your treasure is, there your heart will be also.

Matthew 6:19-21

When we treasure something, we take extra precautions to take care of it. My wedding ring is a treasure. I have had it for over forty years and this band of gold represents a wedding vow to my husband. I wear it with pride and look at it often. I take extra caution when cleaning my treasure. When I remove this ring, I put it in a special place for safe keeping. But, my ring is an earthly treasure and can be lost or stolen.

How do you put treasures in heaven? Nothing that we own on earth will last forever. The only thing that is going to heaven is people. We must invest our lives in people if we are to put treasures in heaven.

If our treasure is in Heaven, it is safe for eternity. Where is your treasure?

✟   Marilyn Phillips

CHOICES

Choose my instruction instead of silver, knowledge rather than choice gold, for wisdom is more precious than rubies, and nothing you desire can compare with her.

Proverbs 8:10-11

71 ✞ ATTITUDE

You were taught, with regard to your former way of life, to put off your old self, which is being corrupted by its deceitful desires; to be made new in the attitude of your minds; and to put on the new self, created to be like God in true righteousness and holiness.

Ephesians 4:22-24

I can be a witness and share about God to all the people around me. This is easy to do when all is well. However, it is very easy when things just aren't going my way to be angry and feel sorry for myself I have Cystic Fibrosis and I am hospitalized frequently which is very disruptive to my life. I have learned that negativity spreads fast and doesn't make anyone feel good. Having a positive attitude regardless of the situation makes everyone feel better and leads to a healthier life.

This verse in Ephesians reminds me that I can always have hope because God has given me a "new self." I have applied this concept during my frequent hospital stays. The hospital staff is actually sad each time when I am finally released from my many hospitalizations. The nurses enjoy being around me because of my God-given joy. When people ask me why I have so much joy, I just tell them that God is my source of happiness.

Your attitude does make a difference! Do you spread negativity to others by your bad moods?

Are people happy or sad when you leave?

✞   Rebekah Phillips

72 ✞ ATTITUDE ADJUSTMENT

"I will give thanks to God with my whole heart."
Psalm 111:1

"Grr! I can't believe he threw his T-shirt into the dirty clothes wrong side out!" Heat rose in my face and my back muscles tightened. I threw the shirt on the floor and stomped to the kid's room. "I bet they did the same thing." Stomp! Stomp! Grumble! Mutter!

My family's dirty clothes habit offended me as if it were a personal attack. Then portions of Colossians 3:17 came to mind. "Do all in the name of the Lord Jesus." I stomped again not quite ready to stop wallowing in my misery.

Not long after that, a thirty-four-year-old friend lost her husband without warning. It was no longer difficult to thank God with each folded T-shirt that my family was intact, and I still had them to put back into those clothes. Soon I began the habit of thanking God for each family member and praying for them as I handled their clothes.

Laundry day presented the opportunity to thank God for the prosperity He had given us. Many people all over the world have trouble finding one set of clothes, and I had several sets to launder right in front of me. On top of that, we were healthy enough to get them dirty and to clean them again.

As I folded each person's clothing, I thanked God for each family member, and asked Him to bless them. Before my laundry was done, gratitude and joy bubbled out of my heart like a washer with too much detergent. It became my special prayer and praise time.

That's just one chore, but the same attitude was applied to each chore at home or at work. Each chore became an opportunity to "whine" or to praise. I recognized that "I" is right in the middle of that word, and if my eyes remained on "I," whining would ensue.

I chose to lift my eyes to the Lord and ask for the supernatural power to follow this scripture. "Whatever you do, whether in word or deed, do it all in the name of the Lord Jesus, giving thanks to God the Father through Him." (Col.3:17) It changed my life from grumble-tude to gratitude.

What attitude are you choosing today?

Prayer:
Father, may we bear fruit in every good work, grow in the knowledge of You, be strengthened with all power according to Your glorious might so that we may have great endurance and patience, and joyfully give thanks to You.
(Personalized Col 1:10-12)

✟   Tamara Roberts

73 ✞ LIVING DIFFERENTLY

So I tell you this, and insist on it in the Lord, that you must no longer live as the Gentiles do, in the futility of their thinking ... You were taught, with regard to your former way of life, to put off your old self, which is being corrupted by its deceitful desires; to be made new in the attitude of your minds; and to put on the new self, created to be like God in true righteousness and holiness.
Ephesians 4:17, 22-24

The moment upon surrendering our hearts to Christ is the moment we are changed ... FOREVER! We are no longer trapped into harmful and deadly lives with unconfessed sin. God sets us free through Christ's love! We have an inner peace and love and goodness in our hearts.

The Holy Spirit will help us live like Christ. As Christians, we have knowledge of how to live a better life. As we study and know more about God, we become more mature in His ways. Christians shouldn't act like non-believers, but as people passionately living for God!

The more we know God, the more we are aware of our sins and old ways of thinking. We know how to love better and to sin less.

Is there an area in your life that is not dedicated to God?

✞   Marilyn Phillips

74 ✞ TAKING CARE

Don't you know that you yourselves are God's temple
and that God's Spirit lives in you?
1 Corinthians 3:16

There are some Bible verses that have encouraged me to take better care of myself despite having Cystic Fibrosis, CF related diabetes and allergies.

The Bible helps me to understand that I am God's temple and God's Spirit lives in me. I am not my own; I was bought at a price. Therefore, I should honor God with my body.

As a Christian, the Holy Spirit lives in me. I need to take care of my body. I should to do everything I can to take care of myself to be healthy. I must have plenty of rest, do all my treatments and take all of my medications. If I don't take care of myself, I will be doing damage to my lungs. This would not honor God and, therefore, hurt my Christian testimony because I wouldn't have the energy to tell others about Christ.

What are the ways you are taking care of your body? The answers can be anything that is helpful! Are you getting enough sleep? Are you eating healthy foods? Do you exercise on a regular basis?

Can you think of ways to improve today?

✞   Rebekah Phillips

75 ✝ CHOOSE TO TRUST

Yet, O LORD, you are our Father.   We are the clay,
you are the potter; we are all the work of your hand.
Isaiah 64:8

As a teenager, I did not choose to trust God's wisdom concerning the many adjustments I had to make. I grew up resentful that my parents had moved me nineteen times before I finished high school. Each time I moved, I was the "new kid" in the class and felt very alone in each school situation. My dream was to one day live in one town, have lots of friends there and never have to adjust to moving again. It never once occurred to me that God had His own plan, and that my having to adjust to new situations and new people would one day be used for His glory.

Many years later I sat in a large circle of ladies, waiting to lead their Bible study. God chose that setting to speak to me about His sovereignty in the circumstances of my life. As I looked around the room in the faces of each lady, I realized I knew every woman's personal story. Each one had confided to me, trusting me to keep confidential what she had shared. God clearly spoke in my mind: "See how I used the adjustments you had to make to prepare you for this? You never meet a stranger, and you have opportunities to meet and love and minister to all kinds of people. The events that you thought were meant for evil were really meant for good!" I was shocked! For the first time I saw how God had been working in my life all of the time.

Have you ever thought about God as a Master Potter of your life? When a potter is preparing clay to be made into a fine vessel, one of the steps he must take is to pound the clay and remove all of the air pockets.

Life has its way of pounding us and removing the impurities. When God is the Master Potter of our lives, He takes every blow this world has designed to destroy and uses it to shape us and turns it into a something beautiful … which is the image of Jesus.

Take a fresh look at the issues in your life that you resent. When placed in the Potter's hands, God uses life's challenges to shape you into something – Someone – very special.

Choose to trust God and He will shape your life to fit His purpose and bring you great joy. Will you trust Him today?

✝ Barbara Christa

76 ✝ CHOICES

The choices we make every day,
Can make or break us along the way.
So many broken people lay in ruin because of choices!
What were they thinking and listening to whose voices?

You hear voices of those who just want to have fun,
And are only looking out for number one.
Their joy and pleasure is very important,
Their desire to be on a high is constant.

Could we say these voices are temptations?
It's been going on for generations.
Their focus on life takes a vacation,
A rest from that stressful situation.

Just a few minutes without worry,
No need for reality, no need to hurry.
But lives fall apart while on vacation from life,
They can't cope; all of a sudden there's strife.

Then there's the voice of truth, from the pages of God's word,
Something inside us is being stirred.
God calls us to be vigilant and focused on life,
Don't listen to those pushing bad choices and strife.

So what can you do if you're led astray?
Ask for God's wisdom, He'll make a way.
Good choices can heal bad choices today,
Listen to God's whisper, don't delay.

✝   ©Beth Peery

77 ✟ CHOOSING YOUR FRIENDS

Do not be misled: "Bad company corrupts good character."

1 Corinthians 15:33

If we want to know who we truly are as a person, look to see who our friends are. You get along with the people who are most similar to you. Do your friends always argue and put others down? Do your friends gossip and lie? Do your friends love and support each other and their family? Do they go to church?

If you associate with people who make bad choices, you will start thinking those choices are okay, and start making those choices as well. The opposite also works – friends that make good choices encourage you to make good choices.

At a student assembly, the minister asked a person to stand on a chair, then he asked two other students to stand on each side of it. He then asked if it would be easier for the student on the chair to pull the other two up, or easier for the two on the floor to pull the one on the chair down. If the one on the chair is a good influence and tries to lift everyone around her it is frequently doomed to failure. It also shows how strong bad influences (represented by the two standing on the floor) can be when they surround us and how they can easily bring us down to their level.

Christians must stand together to hold one another up. Who are the ones surrounding you? Do the people in your life encourage you to make good choices?

✟   Rebekah Phillips

78 ✞ PRAISE

Charm is deceptive, and beauty is fleeting; but a woman who fears the LORD is to be praised.
Proverbs 31:30

Many people think a leader should be pretty and charming just to be popular. However, a true leader chases after God's heart and encourages others to do this same thing. One of the definitions of fear is to have a reverential awe. Reverence means to have honor or respect. Awe means to wonder. This verse says that a woman who honors and respects God and wonders at His glory is to be praised.

Beauty doesn't last forever. We eventually will get older and look older, too. We shouldn't strive to look like models or celebrities to receive praise. Christians should be praised for our love for our great and mighty God.

What do you spend your time doing? Do you spend more time worrying about looking pretty and wearing the most fashionable clothes? Or, do you spend your time reading God's Word, talking to Him, and doing things that bring God glory?

What have you done today to praise God?

✞   Marilyn Phillips

GOD'S FAITHFULNESS

For I am convinced that neither death nor life, neither angels nor demons, neither the present nor the future, nor any powers, neither height nor depth, nor anything else in all creation, will be able to separate us from the love of God that is in Christ Jesus our Lord.

Romans 8:38-39

79 ✞ IMITATORS OF GOD

Be imitators of God, therefore, as dearly loved children and live a life of love, just as Christ loved us and gave himself up for us as a fragrant offering and sacrifice to God.
Ephesians 5:1-2

Our actions and thoughts should reflect the same attitude Jesus had when He was on earth. We are called to glorify God in everything we do in our lives. Christians are called to love others like Jesus does.

This verse reminds me of a trend that was popular when I was a youth. There was this bracelet that had the initials of WWJD. The intials stood for "What Would Jesus Do?" which reminded Christians to ask ourselves this question before we did anything: I loved wearing this bracelet because it helped me to stop and think. For example, if someone made me angry, the bracelet helped remind me not to respond in anger but to address the issue out of love. If I was tempted to gossip, the bracelet reminded me that I needed to keep myself from spreading rumors about others.

This WWJD bracelet helped me to strive to be an imitator of Christ at ALL times.

What are some ways to remind yourself to be an imitator of Christ in all your situations?

✞   Rebekah Phillips

80 ✞ FEARS

I sought the LORD, and he answered me; he delivered me from all my fears.
Psalms 34:4

In 1998, I was diagnosed with Cystic Fibrosis Related Diabetes (CFRD). Having two diseases is an extremely hard crusade. I must have many hours of breathing treatments daily. I was scared because I knew that I had to make decisions that best fit my diseases.

I became more organized with my choices. For example, I cannot easily go out to dinner after seven o'clock. This is especially true during the weekends because the restaurant is crowded and it takes longer to get food, then my blood sugar drops too low. I always can have a snack but my appetite decreases and I can't enjoy dinner. Also, I can't stay out too late because I have to do my breathing treatments on a regular schedule which leaves me exhausted the next day. Balancing health issues and social life is very difficult.

I was afraid of having another disease and additional responsibility. But I was comforted by this Scripture which reminded me to give all my fears to God. God will take my burden! I gave this new health issue to God. Do you understand that your choices today affect your future?

What fears are you facing? Do you realize that God will deliver you from your fears?

✞   Rebekah Phillips

81 ✝ OVERCOMING FEAR

In God, whose word I praise, in the LORD, whose word I praise - in God I trust; I will not be afraid. What can man do to me?
Psalms 56: 10-11

I was very busy during high school with homework, friends, being a cheerleader and having to deal with many hours every day administering breathing treatments due to Cystic Fibrosis.

Sometimes, I felt I never really belonged in a group with my healthy friends because they didn't truly understood what I had to deal with on a daily basis … just to stay healthy.

My high school friends never fully grasped my battle with medical situations. This made me feel lonely and I felt afraid that I would never belong anywhere. The only way I felt connected to someone was when that person had a disease and we could share our fears about our health.

When I read this Psalm, I decided not to be afraid of what others think. I should just focus on what God thinks. God who has given me joy and has given me confidence. I praise God for the confidence that I have in Him.

Do you fear what others think about you? What fears are holding you back from praising God?

✝   Rebekah Phillips

82 ✝ WHERE IS GOD?

Have I not commanded you? Be strong and courageous. Do not be terrified; do not be discouraged, for the LORD your God will be with you wherever you go.

Joshua 1:9

The three of us sat silently in my car, our gazes fixed on the ambulance as my husband was being gurneyed into the emergency vehicle. The quiet was broken by my daughter's friend, Micah. "Why would God do this? Mr. Christa is the finest man I've ever known." In his own way, he expressed the sentiments of mankind through the ages: Where is God when bad things happen? Have you ever asked that question?

Immediately the answer rushed to the forefront of my mind – at least the answer in the case of my husband and our family. I spoke softly, "Micah, yesterday Mr. Christa, Charlcye (our daughter) and I were safe and secure in the palm of God's hand. Do you believe that?"

Although Micah had never placed his faith in God, he had seen evidence of Christ, alive and well, in our lives. "Yes, I believe that," he responded.

I quickly shared, "This morning when our family awoke, Mr. Christa, Charlcye and I were safe and secure in the palm of God's hand. Do you believe that?" "Yes, ma'am," he answered. I shared, "And this very moment, at one p.m. on a Sunday afternoon, with all that is going on, we three are still safe and secure in God's hand. That has not changed. God Has not left us, not even for an instant."

"But Mr. Christa might die!" Micah exclaimed, his eyes filled with confusion and tears. He cared deeply for this Godly man and he feared for David's life.

"Yes, he may die, Micah. God may call David home to Heaven, and if He does, Charlcye and I shall grieve deeply. But if that happens, we both know without a doubt we will continue to be safe and secure in the hand of the One who loves us the most and who will take care of us and lead us. We have no reason to be afraid of what God decides. We will be okay."

The peace I felt that day was based on the assurances I had learned from his Word, the Bible. I trusted completely in God and the promises He has made to us.

Where do you place your trust in the midst of life's trials and losses? Do you have a God who loves you and who has a good plan for your life? One who will never forsake you? Do you live with that certainty every day? Only the God who created us and loves us gives such promises and keeps them.

My husband survived the massive blood clots that nearly drowned him that day, and naturally I am deeply grateful.

That event occurred twenty-four years ago. But each day since that time, he, Charlcye and I have known that every minute of every day of our lives that we have been in the palm of the hand of a loving Father. Do you live with that assurance in your life?

Jesus Christ has made that certainty of Security available to everyone who has fully entrusted his or her life into His care.

When we ask Christ to forgive our sins and to come into our lives, we give ourselves over to Him, trusting Him to meet our needs in every circumstance. He becomes our Provider, our Safe Place, our Security, our Savior (the One who paid for our sins) and our Lord (Master, Owner, Boss). He is with us in the brightest of days and in the darkest of nights.

Isaiah 43:2-3 says, *"When you pass through the waters, I will be with you; and when you pass through the rivers, they will not sweep over you. When you walk through the fire, you will not be burned; the flames will not set you ablaze. For I am the Lord your God, the Holy One of Israel, your Savior."*

God is with His children regardless of the trials and sufferings of this life. He will help us through each of them.

Will you choose to place your security in Jesus Christ today?

✝ Barbara Christa

83 ✟ NOTHING IS TOO HARD FOR GOD

I am the LORD, the God of all mankind. Is anything too hard for me?
Jeremiah 32:27

Often when in a difficult situation, we tend to think that God just isn't big enough for the tasks and doesn't even know what is going on in our lives. For instance, when I was looking for a job to return to teaching at age fifty, I thought that God had simply forgotten about me.

Maybe it was just too difficult for God to provide a job for a fifty year-old woman. I went to numerous interviews but the competition was great and it seemed like younger applicants were always chosen.

A friend, Linda Whitten, asked her principal to interview me. The interview went great and, I was hired to teach second grade. This principal, Mike Dukes, was a former pastor. Years later, when I had breast cancer, God used this Christian principal to encourage my heart as he prayed for me. Mike made sure my class was covered while I left early to go to radiation treatments for six grueling weeks.

God didn't just have a job, God had the perfect job for me, I just had to be patient! God is so great and so mighty.

Are you facing a difficult situation? Is there anything too hard for God?

✟   Marilyn Phillips

84 ✟ GOD WILL FIGHT FOR YOU

The LORD will fight for you; you need only to be still.

Exodus 14:14

This Bible verse promises that the LORD will fight for me; I need only to be still. This verse stood out to me when I was reading how God helped Moses, despite the many trials, to lead the Israelites out of Egypt to a safer place. I understood that God has helped my parents accept the fact that I had Cystic Fibrosis (CF) which is a devastating disease.

As I grew up, I realized that God would lead me through many trials in my life. God will take care of my needs as long as I follow Him. Letting the Lord fight for me in all of my troubles has really helped me because I don't have to do anything but to stand still.

There were times when I fought for myself and I was drained. Sometimes I felt like giving up when I fought the battle against CF by myself. I was exhausted from standing up. When I learned to let go and let the Lord fight for me, I had nothing to worry about.

God is constantly looking out for me and fighting to protect me. When I let God lead me and fight for me, I am full of energy and have peace when troubles come my way. God has fought for me in the past and has given me confidence to face anything in the future.

Are you letting God fight for you in every area of your life?

✟   Rebekah Phillips

85 ✟ THANKFULNESS

Always giving thanks to God the Father for everything, in the name of our Lord Jesus Christ.
Ephesians 5:20

One November years ago, on each day leading to Thanksgiving I listed at least one thing for which I was thankful. Next, I gave the praise to God for the blessings for which I was thankful on that particular day. Some days, I could list many things I was thankful for, but others days I struggled to find only a few things over which to express thankfulness.

On Thanksgiving Day, I looked at all the things I had listed and I gave thanks to God for what He had given me. I realized how blessed I was, and that most people didn't have these things I was thankful for – such as a loving family that lives nearby, good health, the gift of eternal life and the freedom to worship God, a college degree, a teaching job, and so much more!

This exercise made me think about how often I take things for granted. Now, I do my best to be thankful for something each day - even in a bad situation. A bad situation can teach me something if I look for the lesson.

I encourage you to write down what you are thankful for every day for a week. You may be surprised at how much you are blessed by God.

Why not start your thankfulness list today?

✟   Rebekah Phillips

86 ✝ IT WAS A GOD THING

Delight yourself in the LORD and he will give you the desires of your heart.
Psalms 37:4

It's easy to give God credit for the "BIG" things that happen in our lives such as safety in a storm, healing from an illness, etc. But I am convinced God is even in the "little" things in our lives. God cares about the 'desires of our hearts.'

I had been grieving my cock-a-poo for 4 years. She had come to live with us when my aunt and uncle moved to an assisted living facility. She was a part of our family for over twelve years. I had no desire to replace her with another dog. Yet, I truly longed for the companionship of a little lap dog. I did not share these feelings with anyone. Although my husband knew how I felt, no one else in my circle of family and friends did.

One day I told my husband I was going to start looking for a little rescue dog. He was excited for me and tried to help by scouring the Internet for possibilities.

Within a few days I had seen dozens of candidates at nearby animal shelters and rescue groups. Now it was time to go meet some of these little ones in need of a forever home. Still no one other than my husband knew I was looking for a little dog.

I visited three different shelters and met some sweet little dogs; but I did not bring home any of them. I just couldn't do it. How could I pick one dog and leave the rest? Leaving each shelter empty handed was heart wrenching.

Then one morning I was thinking about the shelter visits, I stopped and said out loud, "I can't do this anymore! I am done. If God wants me to have a little dog, He'll have to drop one in my lap because I am not going to another shelter."

Two hours later I receive a phone call from my daughter-in-law. Her mother insisted she call me. My sweet daughter-in-law apologizes before saying any more. I tell her it's OK and to give me the message. Her mother had a friend with a 10-month-old puppy who needed a home. I laughed out loud. God had heard me and was giving me a dog.

When people ask about my little schnauzer-mix lap dog I tell them, "It was a God Thing." Then I explain to them how God dropped her in my lap.

Do you have an unspoken request or a yearning in your heart? Make a habit of delighting in Lord Jesus.

✝ Anita Barngrover

87 ✝ BLOOD OF JESUS

But if we walk in the light, as he is in the light, we have fellowship with one another, and the blood of Jesus, his Son, purifies us from all sin ... If we confess our sins, he is faithful and just and will forgive us our sins and purify us from all unrighteousness.

I John: 1:7, 9

In February of 2014, I went into the hospital diagnosed with kidney disease and an e-coli infection in my blood that was resistant to the normal antibiotics I had already tried. In order to treat this infection in my blood, I needed super antibiotics piped directly into my blood every twelve hours for eleven days.

After five days in the hospital, I was allowed to go home with the agreement that I would continue this intra-venous treatment every twelve hours at home for the remaining six days. A PICC-line was inserted into a vein in my left arm and threaded upward about eight inches directly to my heart to be sure the medication reached my whole body. Twice a day for about an hour I was connected to a long tube on a pole as life giving medication was infused into my veins ... one drop at a time.

I had never been seriously ill before, and this was an experience that caused me to think a little differently than I ever had before. On the day I arrived home, my husband handed me a compact disc on which were copied songs my music minister at church wanted me to hear and study.

Our music ensemble at church, in which I play a keyboard, would be using these songs for praise and worship during the next couple of months. So I began to listen, but I only listened to two of the ten songs.

The second one was called "The Blood." The words of this song shared the message that the blood of Jesus took my guilt away and replaced it with forgiveness; it protects me from the powers of darkness, conquers the fear of death, and much, much more.

I had been thinking nearly non-stop about my own blood for several days now, and as I listened to a recounting of things that the blood of Jesus has done and continues to do for me, I wept in gratitude and humility. My blood was poisoned, but the blood of my Savior, Jesus, was pure and precious, and able to heal me. And oh, how I needed healing.

I thought of the verse in I John that says "the blood of Jesus cleanses me from all my sin," and again I thanked Jesus for taking away my sin and giving me life and peace with God. I was reminded that the blood of Jesus that takes away my sin to give me spiritual health is the same blood that allows me to have healing in my physical blood. I owe everything that is good in my life to Jesus who willingly gave his blood for my salvation and healing.

I am so thankful for the blood of Jesus. Do you realize that Jesus shed His precious blood for you?

✞   Sue King

88 ✞ CAN I BE SEPARATED?

For I am convinced that neither death nor life, neither angels nor demons, neither the present nor the future, nor any powers, neither height nor depth, nor anything else in all creation, will be able to separate us from the love of God that is in Christ Jesus our Lord.

Romans 8:38-39

Have you ever felt lonely and isolated? Have you ever felt you are separated from God and facing battles on your own?

The Bible promises that nothing can separate you from God's love. If you have asked Christ to be your Savior and Lord then you can claim this promise!

Often, when my daughter is extremely sick with CF and hospitalized, it is so easy to feel alone. Sometimes I let fear and worry consume my thoughts. But, God promises that He is with me. On the way to and from the hospital, I pray. I feel God's presence and I'm overcome with God's love.

When are the times you are most challenged and you feel abandoned?

Do you know that God is with you at all times?

✞   Marilyn Phillips

89 ✝ WITHOUT COMPLAINING

Do everything without complaining or arguing.
Philippians 2:14

In 2011, one of my frequent hospital stays was the most challenging time I had ever experienced. My kidneys began quickly shutting down due to a reaction to a medication. All I wanted to do was sit still so that I wouldn't feel sick to my stomach when I moved. I was put on a special diet to help my kidneys. Due to the nausea and a limited bland diet, I barely ate and lost weight.

My kidneys were almost to the point of requiring dialysis. Apparently, there was little to be done but to wait and see if my kidneys would heal themselves. I was so discouraged. I decided to obey God and *do everything without complaining or arguing*. Romans 12:12 says to be joyful always and be thankful. God is always active in those who are faithful. James 1:2-4 reminded me that trials can sharpen anyone's faith. I wanted to live out these verses because they helped me to tell others about God.

I determined to be more positive and joyful to the people around me during these difficult trials Some nurses even told me that my joyful attitude helped them have a better day. Also, nurses take me seriously when I do complain. I encourage you to choose a positive attitude. Having a joyful heart helps you to overcome anything!

The source of my joy is God! He can be yours too! How can you be thankful, or positive, in your trials?

✝ Rebekah Phillips

90 ✝ FORTRESS

He who fears the LORD has a secure fortress, and for his children it will be a refuge.
Proverbs 14:26

I am picking up my granddaughters from school today. While waiting in a long, double line of cars I have plenty of time to think. In order to be a member of this coveted line, I have to arrive at the school at least twenty minutes early. Those arriving later don't make it into the school parking lot. So I wait, watching the frustrated parents and grandparents who are stuck on the street waiting their turn to get in line. It's a traffic nightmare!

While waiting, I remembered back to a simpler, quieter end to school days … my school days. When I got out of school there was no one waiting to chauffeur the children home. The only rush was to walk away from the building as fast as we could. Some of my best childhood memories are from those walks home from school with my friends. The walks were always leisurely and fun with a lot of laughter and giggling – with no adults around. It was our time.

Sometimes we would stop at the local drug store to purchase a treat. Our favorites were frozen Peanut Butter Cups or Snickers candy bars for a nickel. Or, we could get a fountain Coke in a little glass for a nickel. We would laugh, talk, and have fun for a few minutes. Then we'd continue our trek home. Some of us went east and others went west from downtown to get to their homes. Some even had to go back toward the school to get to home. And the rest of us headed south. It wasn't a pack of kids walking home. It was more of a steady stream of pairs or groups of three or four.

Those of us headed south had a longer walk; and we had to cross the only paved road through town. It was a busy state highway; but busy didn't mean then what it does now. Those of us headed south were really lucky because we got to walk through our town's City Park. This meant another stop. Sometimes we would use the playground equipment. Other times we would just sit on the picnic tables and talk. You see, when we got home, that was it for talking to our friends until the next day. We did have telephones; but kids didn't use them just to talk to other kids. Oh, no ... that never occurred to us. The telephone was used only by adults and only as a necessity. So, we never hurried home from school.

Suddenly, the movement of children exiting the school building brought me back from memories of my childhood to today's reality. And, I sit here waiting for my granddaughters and realize these children will never know the freedoms I had in childhood. Their world is much more complicated and dangerous. Where is their security? I pray for my grandchildren's safety from the evil in our world. I pray for their parents. May they daily build a secure fortress, a strong and secure place, for their families.

Are you building a secure fortress for your family?

✝   Anita Barngrover

91 ✝ GOD STRENGTHENS YOU

For the eyes of the LORD range throughout the earth to strengthen those whose hearts are fully committed to him.

2 Chronicles 16:9a

Often, we are overcommitted with activities due to time constraints! We can only do so much in 24 hours each day.

Developing friendships, being involved in church activities and doing the best job at work takes time. In addition, we need to grocery shop and prepare meals for our families each day. What is difficult is the fact that all of the activities are good things.

Are you committed to doing a good job enough to sacrifice the time required? Is your heart really in it?

God looks for our "heart attitude" to determine if we are committed to doing His will. It's harder than it sounds. Being committed to God means that we are willing to invest the time necessary to accomplish God's will ... and with an attitude that is pleasing to God.

It takes time to read the Bible and pray. Is your heart fully committed to doing God's will?

✝   Marilyn Phillips

92 ✝ HONOR GOD

Love the LORD your God with all your heart and with all your soul and with all your strength."
Deuteronomy 6:5

On Mother's Day 1979, my husband and I were sitting in the back row of our church. Married for eight years, we were parents of two active boys with another on the way. We loved being parents to our boys. Life was never dull! We were always on the run. If we weren't going to baseball, soccer, or basketball practices and games we were busy with church outreach programs, group campouts, or going to the doctor's office for a variety of ailments, sprains or breaks. Now, I can honestly say I had never thought about our lives changing. I guess I didn't consider the future because I was just too involved in the now. But I loved every minute of our busy, exciting life and was so proud of my boys. I had not considered the fact they would grow up and actually leave us some day. I really didn't want to think about my children leaving and living on their own.

Our pastor got up to speak after a beautiful service of singing and worshiping our God. Since it was Mother's Day, I sat there expecting the normal sermon about how precious mothers are to all of us. But this day, Pastor Hal Brooks had a message from God that changed the direction of our parenting. Nearly forty years later, my husband and I still remember that message: Too many children were being raised to be dependent on momma. I wonder now if the pastor had recently been involved in some challenging counseling sessions. Pastor Brooks drove home the point that if we loved our children, we needed to raise them to leave home. Well, that was a new way of thinking for me.

Together, my husband and I vowed that day to raise independent children who could leave home one day. It wasn't always easy. My husband and I had to remind each other of our promise to God that day on many different occasions over the years. Like all parents of young children, we were very busy. Each of our boys had household chores. We did not pay our children for these chores. Chores were just a part of being in a family. As they got older, our boys were paid for projects around the house above and beyond their individual chores.

We set the tone in our house with high expectations for our boys. We believed doing so would build a strong foundation for each son. They frequently heard, "Always do your best. Be polite and respectful at all times. Work hard. Be kind. And above all else, Love the Lord your God with all your heart, with all your soul, and with all your strength." And we made certain our boys had experiences to reinforce our words. We read the Bible out loud in our home. We prayed. We attended church. We worked on church and community outreach programs together as a family.

It wasn't easy, but after high school graduation and leaving for college, three boys grew up to be strong independent men who gave us three beautiful daughters-in-law and seven super grandkids. And guess what? All three sons and their families live nearby. We believe God rewarded our vow to raise independent children by blessing us now with their nearness.

Are you training children in your family to seek and honor God?

✞   Anita Barngrover

ACTIONS

But someone will say, "You have faith; I have deeds."
Show me your faith without deeds, and I will show
you my faith by what I do ... As the body without the
spirit is dead, so faith without deeds is dead.
James 2:18, 26

93 ✝ GOD CHOSE YOU

You did not choose me, but I chose you and appointed you to go and bear fruit – fruit that will last. Then the Father will give you whatever you ask in my name.

John 15:16

Adopted children are chosen. My niece, Valerie, and her husband, James, just spent one and half years in the adoption process. Finally, they traveled to Korea from Texas to get their baby boy, Seth!

This vivacious child, Seth, now has all the rights that go along with being in a family. Seth has three older sisters who adore him and we can't imagine life without this active little boy.. He's part of our family now. Seth will always know that his parents went to great lengths to get him. He was chosen!

Did you know that God chose you to be His child? You are adopted into His family. God not only chose you but God has a purpose for you to bear fruit. By sharing your faith, God will use you to bring others to the saving grace of Jesus Christ.

What kind of fruit are you bearing today?

✝   Marilyn Phillips

94 ✞ GOD'S AGENDA

"Be wise in the way you act toward outsiders; make the most of every opportunity. Let your conversation be always full of grace, seasoned with salt, so that you may know how to answer everyone.

Colossians 4:5b-6.

When I leave the house for appointments or errands, my husband knows I will not return quickly. God and I have an agenda.

Usually before the car leaves the garage, I pray that God will give me His words and an opportunity to speak His truth to someone I will encounter that day. I purposefully allow extra time while I'm away from home to talk with people, engage them in conversation, give a word of encouragement, or even pray with them. Some encounters are short. Others are longer and with a stranger that I may never see again. The depth of our conversation depends on the amount of time available to share, as well as the prompting of the Holy Spirit. My ultimate purpose is to share the hope I have found in Jesus Christ.

Initially I try to connect with someone through eye contact and a cheerful "Hello!" at grocery stores, the local produce market, or other shops I frequent. Over time, with familiar faces, our short conversations stem from casual comments, to discussions about their family or new events, and then, to longer, more personal conversations concerning problems, difficulties, and even their hopelessness. It is a joy for me to hear about their lives and listen to their problems. You see, I learn their names and try to develop relationships, if possible, so they will know I REALLY care about their concerns. At the end of each visit, I leave them with a Bible verse that applies to our discussion or an uplifting thought that is focused on the hope we have in Jesus.

Eventually all my conversations lead to sharing the Good News ... how the Creator God made them, cares about every detail of their life, and has a plan for them; how God sent His Son, Jesus Christ, to this Earth to die on the cross to save them from their sins. I share that Jesus was raised from the dead and ascended to Heaven where He lives and prays for us. I want them to know HE is the ONE TRUE LIVING GOD who is alive and actively working in people's lives, and who will return to this world one day to make everything right. I believe that God will use the spiritual seeds planted to bring glory to His name.

I've heard the comment from several pastors and missionaries that it can take up to seven times for the gospel to be presented to an individual before he or she will make the all-important decision to make Christ the Lord of his or her life. God can use just one seed that's planted. Those seeds add up when they are sewn in the hearts of those who don't know our Savior.

It's not our responsibility to lead that person to faith in Jesus. God tells us to plant the seeds of faith. It's His responsibility to water those seeds, to grow someone's faith and bring them to His saving grace.

Many people I connect with ask me why I would care about their needs and their eternal future. That leads to the reason I love life and have hope and a bright future. I know what Jesus has done for me personally. The seed I plant as I share my faith may be the first time someone has heard God's Good News or it may be the seventh time. It's exciting and thrilling to know I am partnering with my Lord, the

Almighty God of this universe to share the hope that is within me.

God commands us to share His Good News about Jesus, so I want to be obedient to His command.   In Mark Cahill's book, *One Thing You Can't Do in Heaven,* he tells that being 'really cool' is going to heaven when you die and bringing a whole lot of people with you."

I want to "make the most of every opportunity" so others will spend Eternity with their Creator and Savior. Time is short!   There is much work to be done.   Go make a difference in someone's life for eternity!

Will you recognize God's agenda and be available to share His message with someone who so desperately needs Him?

✝   Jane Weaver

95 ✟ COMPLETE TASKS

Therefore go and make disciples of all nations, baptizing them in the name of the Father and of the Son and of the Holy Spirit, and teaching them to obey everything I have commanded you. And surely I am with you always, to the very end of the age."
Matthew 28:19-20

Christians have the security of eternity in Heaven. It's a promise we can claim. Because it is in the Bible, we can believe that we are required as Christians to teach, obey, and share God's Words.

The Bible promises that our sins are forgiven and removed far from us. Why does God leave us here? He could just take us on to heaven when we trust Him, but He has a task for each of us. We have security – the world needs security – our reason for security should be shared. We have the task of testifying about our great and mighty God.

Are you sharing the information that can change the eternal destination of your friends and family? What if God has put a person into your life specifically for you to share God's grace and mercy? It could be a cashier, waitress, or a family member.

If you don't share about God, who will?

What person can you testify to about God's grace today?

✟   Marilyn Phillips

96 ✞ GO TELL

See these lost people – they're all around you,
You may not know them, but I do.

Who are the Lost? They are in the next car,
They're next in line at the store, that's who they are.

Family, strangers, could be your best friend,
They're lost, that's what matters in the end.

But I knew them before they were born,
I know when they're happy, I know when they mourn.

I know their thoughts and words before spoken,
They are lost and my heart is broken.

I love them!

Who will tell them about my love?
Who will tell about my Son from above?

Who came down to earth to save them
From the one prowling for souls to condemn?

Who will be my hands and feet?
Who will be my voice on the street?

I don't want ONE of these to be lost,
For I've paid the ultimate cost.

On a cruel cross, my only begotten Son died,
Eternal life, for believers, will not be denied.

Will you be the one?
Will you tell the lost about my Son?

I know it sounds scary,
But do not tarry.

I'll give you courage and words – all you need to know,
For telling the Lost – now please go!

I love them!

✞ ©Beth Peery

97 ✝ GOD'S WAYS

As the heavens are higher than the earth, so are my ways higher than your ways and my thoughts than your thoughts."
Isaiah 55:8

God came down and glory filled a small concrete one-room hut that we visited on the third day of a recent mission trip in Zambia. I feel a little like Mary Magdalene must have felt after she witnessed Jesus' resurrection when I think back. Compelled to share with anyone willing to listen, I too have been forever changed.

Before jumping into the experience, I should back track and explain a little about the first two days, and why I was in Africa. Along with eight other team members affiliated with Evangelism Partners International, our goal was to help construct a building for a church that had been planted several years earlier which had been meeting in a small school.

We were to go door-to-door to share the gospel by using an EvangeCube® which is a witnessing tool with seven graphic panels that present the Gospel of Jesus Christ and we were to invite people to the new church. Each team member had interpreters. God blessed me with a highly dedicated group of strangers to walk along beside me. Mine were Cecilia and Given. Cecilia walked seven hours each day to be with us and then walked another seven hours home until we found out and began giving her rides back home. Given, who always had a smile on his face, was also willing to pay the sacrifice by walking two or three hours and leaving his family to be a part of our group. Sensing God's call and timing even though they were members of churches far away, they were willing to block out eight days to help.

Because of their unselfishness, we decided to drive to their neighborhoods during the second week. I got to speak at Cecilia's church and our ladies group performed some storytelling skits and songs for her home church one afternoon the second week, so we were able to minister to three churches instead of just one due to Cecilia's and Given's obedience to the call of the Christ.

Each day before we left, we would pray and ask the Lord to guide our steps and to set divine appointments for us. On the first day, we shared with about fourteen people and eight prayed to receive Christ. I was so happy and excited; I literally jumped for joy when a girl named Gift, the first person we shared with, prayed to receive Christ. The first day was great; the people were gracious, warm, welcoming, and ready for harvest. Enthusiastic as we walked back to the church cite, we praised God for such a great day. I told Cecilia and Given to pray that the Lord would give us ten professions of faith the next day. The next day, we went out again and fourteen people prayed to receive Christ. Again, we were overjoyed by God's faithfulness. On the walk back that second day, I said, "Tomorrow we need to ask God for twenty people to pray to receive Christ." Cecilia shook her head and said, "No, we need to ask for forty."

I laughed nervously a bit worried about how we could get so many professions in a few hours, like the results were up to me instead of the Lord, and said, "Okay." Driven, the next day, we were determined to reach our goal, knowing it would be challenging, but confident we could. We went to many houses and when we shared we always asked if they could invite some friends or other family members to listen to our presentation to help pump up our numbers, but it seemed like just about everyone we talked to had either made a decision or wanted to debate which day of the week we should worship.

I was feeling pressured that we weren't going to make our goal and time was running out. We headed to a four-plex which looked hopeful that we could share with a lot of people in a relatively short amount of time. At the time, I hate to admit it, but I was fixated on meeting our magic number more than anything else. The first three people on the end of the building had already made professions, so we moved on hurriedly.

An elderly woman stepped out of her small dwelling and asked if we would come inside to share with her. She had seen our EvangeCube® and was intrigued. We were thrilled to have the open invitation, so we walked inside and quickly began our presentation. At the end, we asked if she wanted to ask Jesus in her heart. She said she had already done that. I have to admit, I was glad she was saved, but foolishly, I was a little disappointed that she had already made a profession of faith because we were a long way from our goal and time was almost up.

Wanting to mask my disappointment, I asked her if there was anything we could pray with her about, and she said she had six daughters and granddaughters that weren't married and asked if we would pray for them to marry good men. We agreed and prayed. Surprising myself, I felt prompted to show her pictures of my family which I had brought with me. Quickly, I showed her my small photo album but slowed down when I came to a picture of Macey, who is our three-year-old miracle grandchild.

Macey was born with the umbilical cord wrapped around her neck and as a result, oxygen was cut off to her brain for a while. She had a hard time learning to walk. For over two years she scooted around on her bottom and never crawled. Many specialists saw her; she had numerous tests and countless hours of physical therapy. Some said she would never walk except with crutches, but God miraculously healed her. While I was telling the grandmother Macey's story, a little girl came scooting through the open doorway on her bottom just the way that Macey used to get around.

The timing was divine. I asked the grandmother who the little girl was. She said she was her granddaughter, Elizabeth, who was seven years old. After a few questions, she told us that Elizabeth had never walked or stood up and that the doctors couldn't help her. We asked if we could pray for her. She gratefully agreed.

I can't explain it, but it was as if heaven opened up. In true Zambian fashion, we all started praying at the same time for Elizabeth. Resurrection power filled the room. It was unlike anything I have ever experienced before. With faith and hope in my heart, I asked Given to ask Elizabeth if she could stand up. With trusting eyes, she grabbed hold to my fingertips and stood straight and tall, not wobbly like you might expect when someone was standing for the first time. We all clapped, praised God, and rejoiced. I suspect there were angels all around her holding her little legs for support.

Elizabeth walked around the room going from person to person then back to me. It was amazing. Firsthand, I witnessed a miracle. Round and round the room the small cherub toddled about three or four times. I could tell she was tiring, but before the magical moment was over, I whispered, "Elizabeth, do you think you can walk to me with no one helping you?"

With bated breath, we paused; everyone's eyes totally fixed on the small girl. With the escort of unseen angels, she walked steadily toward me. I trembled inside at the incredible joy and privilege of seeing heaven brought to earth right before my very eyes. We didn't make our goal of forty salvations that day which was our plan; instead we got to experience God's plan which was so much more awesome. Isaiah 55:6 says, "For my thoughts are not your thoughts, neither are your ways, my ways." It's true; God's ways are far beyond anything I could imagine.

✝   Carolyn Hedgecock

98 ✟ ACTIONS PORTRAY YOUR FAITH

But someone will say, "You have faith; I have deeds."
Show me your faith without deeds, and I will show
you my faith by what I do .. As the body without the
spirit is dead, so faith without deeds is dead.
James 2:18, 26

There are so many people that proclaim to be Christians but their actions show that they really are not. These so-called Christians act like non-believers even though they claim to be a Christian. Because of this sad fact, many non-believers won't ever attend church or give their life to Christ.

The Bible even says in James 2:19 that demons believe that there is a God and they shudder! So, just because someone says they believe there is a God ... doesn't mean that they understand the nature of God.

As Christians, our faith should dictate our actions. We cannot have one without the other. If we say we love others, we should act like we love others instead of tearing them down. If we love others then we should share about God's plan for salvation.

Do your actions portray what you believe?

What have you done today to show a friend at work or a family member that you are a Christian?

✟   Marilyn Phillips

99 ✞ ACTION

For we are God's workmanship, created in Christ Jesus to do good works, which God prepared in advance for us to do.
Ephesians 2:10

We often wonder what God has planned for us. I have recently heard, "I wish I had a crystal ball that would magically show my future to me." Or, friends have commented that they would like to know how a decision would affect life before making the decision.

Much time and energy are focused on which decisions to make involving our future: what college to attend or which profession to choose. Whom should we date or marry? Where should we live? Should we have children?

Perhaps focusing on God's plan for today is just as important as the future. We tend to think that today's activities do not even affect the future. However, did you know that God has prepared works for us to do EACH day, and God has equipped us with everything we need to accomplish His will daily.

The Biblical principle is: the person who is faithful in small things will be rewarded with greater responsibility (read Luke 19:17). Are you faithful in the small things God calls you to do?

What is God calling you to do today that will minister to others and point them to God?

✞   Marilyn Phillips

But in your hearts set apart Christ as Lord. Always be prepared to give an answer to everyone who asks you to give the reason for the hope that you have. But do this with gentleness and respect, keeping a clear conscience, so that those who speak maliciously against your good behavior in Christ may be ashamed of their slander.

1 Peter 3:15-16

This verse says to ALWAYS be ready to share your faith! People will see you as someone different if you are a Christian who is constantly faithful to God. Your actions show what you believe.

On many occasions, people in my life ask me why I am so happy. Even at the grocery store I frequent, the cashier has told me that my face always has a smile. Depending on the situation, I talk about God and how He always makes me happy and has blessed my life.

Many times, a nurse will notice my cheerful heart when I am in the hospital when I am very sick with Cystic Fibrosis complications. This gives me an opportunity to share my faith. We need to be ready at ALL times to give our testimony in one minute or be able to have a long detailed discussion.

Have you thought through your testimony? Have you written it down? Can you give a quick version in one minute?

✞   Rebekah Phillips

101 ✟ LET YOUR LIGHT SHINE FOR JESUS

In the same way, let your light shine before men, that they may see your good deeds and praise your Father in heaven.

Matthew 5:16

A small candle when lit will light up a room. Have you ever had a candlelit dinner? Many churches use candles at services. You can even see a small candle in a large, dark sanctuary.

Have you ever been to a Christmas or New Year's candlelight service where everyone's candle is lit in turn from one small candle? The resulting glow is inspiring. Light makes the unseen visible. We can share the light with others.

Our light is a reflection of Jesus Christ. This light shows brightly when we are kind and considerate to others. Basically, it is loving our neighbors as ourselves and realizing that God has created all.

Does your light make Jesus more visible to others? What can you do today so that others can see the light of Jesus Christ?

✟   Marilyn Phillips

102 ✝ A SHINING LIGHT

"You are the light of the world. A city on a hill cannot be hidden. Neither do people light a lamp and put it under a bowl. Instead they put it on its stand, and it gives light to everyone in the house. In the same way, let your light shine before men, that they may see your good deeds and praise your Father in heaven."
Matthew 5: 14-16

What can I say to my dearest friend who has just been informed by doctors that she has only weeks to live? That question torments my soul. How can the cancer invading her body have progressed so rapidly? A surgeon removed a huge tumor and three-fourths of Paddi's stomach in hopes of prolonging her life. It didn't work! My friend is only forty-two. She has four precious children and a husband, Mike, who desperately need her.

Upon hearing the tragic news, I immediately call Paddi. She asks me to come to the hospital. My husband, Nolan, and I quickly prepare for the trip from Fort Worth to Tulsa. As Nolan and I travel we listen to Christian music. My heart is heavy. I can't speak without crying. Memories flood my mind. Paddi is a wonderful mother and enjoys home schooling her children. Mike adores Paddi. Through the years, we have shared birthday parties, holidays, and Christmas. Paddi always had a New Year's Eve Party for families and we prayed in the New Year.

Nolan sees the hospital and parks. I start crying again. How can I see Paddi knowing she may die soon? Grief presses in so heavily that I feel nauseous. I can't walk. Nolan puts his arm around me as I try to regain my composure. We slowly go through the hospital entrance.

I expect to see a depressing scene when I enter the room. But, I am surprised! Paddi is dressed in overalls and a bright T-shirt. She looks beautiful with sparkling eyes and a radiant smile. She has a tube in her throat making speaking difficult. We embrace. Over twenty friends and relatives have gathered to be near our dying friend. Doctors offer no hope.

Paddi wants to talk with each of us but it is impossible to do so in her small hospital room. She calls the nurse and insists on going outside to a park downstairs. The nurse gently unhooks numerous tubes from monitors so Paddi can have a few moments of freedom but she must return to her room in forty-five minutes for the next IV. With much determination, Paddi refuses to ride in a wheel chair and triumphantly walks downstairs and across the street to the park. It is chilly but wonderful weather. Paddi hasn't been outside in days. She is exhilarated. Family and friends follow slowly and help Paddi to a nearby picnic table.

We sit closely together on the picnic bench to keep warm from the cool breeze. Paddi smiles bravely and speaks confidently despite the tube in her throat. She says, "Mike and I want to share with all of you about the wonderful things that God is doing in our life right now. I know that you all are hurting because I may soon die. We have all lost people that we love. God has given Scripture to minister to Mike and my family and I want God to be glorified in everything I say and do. One verse in particular, "*My Grace is sufficient for thee,*" (II Corinthians 12:9) is true in our lives. We have discovered that God's grace is sufficient to meet our every need. And my dear friends, God's grace is here for you today and will comfort you if I die soon."

We are all amazed that Paddi can minister to our aching hearts even though she is in so much pain. My friend has an IV attached to a pain medicine dispenser. With the push of a button, Paddi can have momentary relief from the intense pain.

Mike continues, "Paddi, has always said that if anything happens that I would have to die first because I depend on Paddi for so much. We all know about Paddi's strong faith. But during the last few months, God has helped me to become strong. I don't want Paddi to die and I am praying for a miracle, but I want God's name to be glorified in everything we say and do." Mike wept and so did we. I have never seen Mike stand so tall.

Paddi begins speaking softly; "I don't want to leave Mike, my precious children, my parents, or my friends. But if I die soon, I know God will give all of you the strength for today and courage for tomorrow that you need. God knows what is best for me and for my family. The Bible says in Philippians 1:21, *"To live is Christ and to die is gain."* I believe God's promises with all my heart. I know that Heaven is wonderful and we will all be together again one day in the presence of our Lord and Savior." We all smile through our tears.

The forty-five minutes are soon over so we must return to the hospital. Reluctantly, our group slowly walks back to the room. The nurse is there to administer medication as soon as Paddi arrives. My brave friend is exhausted, so we encourage her to take a nap and promise we will all stay until she awakens. We wait in the hall. Her nap lasted only fifteen minutes due to intense pain.

Soon it is time for us to go back to Fort Worth. But how can I leave and say "Good-bye" knowing that I may never see Paddi alive again? Nolan and I enter the room. I sit near Paddi and we hug each other tightly. Uncontrollable tears stream down my face as we embrace. I cry, "Oh, Paddi, I can't leave you." She says, "I love you, Marilyn. God is with you. Always remember to "Let your light so shine before men that they may see your good works and glorify your Father which is in Heaven." (Matthew 5:16) With a final embrace I whisper, "Your light is shining!"

Nolan and I leave the hospital. Finally, I understand that Paddi is a living testimony to the power of Jesus Christ. Her life has been spent being a Godly wife and nurturing her children. My precious friend can glorify God despite intense pain because of her strong faith. She openly shares her faith with friends, doctors, and nurses. I am even more aware of God's sovereignty. What a great and mighty God we have who can give comfort and peace to a young woman facing cancer and an uncertain future.

I wrote about the events on the way home knowing that this must be published so others will know about the power of God. I sent the article to Paddi, she read it and gave me permission to share about her life.

Days later, we received the dreaded call. At the funeral, Paddi's family and friends gave wonderful testimonies. God's grace was flowing. Paddi had spent her life as a living testimony to the power of Jesus Christ. After Paddi's death, I was even more aware of the sovereignty of our mighty God who gave a young dying woman PEACE and comfort to her family and friends. Even in death, my friend taught me an everlasting lesson about God.

Is the light of Christ shining in your life?

✞   Marilyn Phillips

103 ✝ MINISTRY

I can do everything through Him who gives me strength!

Phillipians 4:13

I was blessed to grow up in a small town farming community. My Mom took me to church every Sunday. When I was ten and a half years old, I accepted Jesus Christ as my Saviour on an Easter Sunday morning, a day I shall always remember!

I knew God had a plan and a purpose for my life. I wasn't sure what it was until many years later.

I attended Baylor University and married my Freshmen year to the love of my life, Duane. We have been married for 53 wonderful years and God blessed us with a son and a daughter, seven grandchildren and seven wonderful great-grandchildren. We raised our family in a Christian home and taught them about Jesus at an early age.

In my early fifties, I felt God calling me to devote more time to women's ministry and I began to do that at the church where we were members.

Today, I volunteer as a Christian Women's Job Corps (CWJC) Certified Site Coordinator and love working with the women I serve through that ministry. The ladies attend sessions for six weeks that include: daily Bible Study, interview skills, computer training, work place appearance, body language skills, lifestyle management skills, resume preparation and finally graduation.

God has blessed and opened doors for me through that ministry. I love sharing about the CWJC program and how it blesses and transforms women's lives and prepares them with life skills. I feel I am, at last, serving where God wants me to.

I am so grateful to God for opening that door of ministry opportunity for me!

Are you seeking God's ministry for you? Do you believe that God will give you the strength?

✞   Lynda Swoveland

For I was hungry and you gave me something to eat, I was thirsty and you gave me something to drink, I was a stranger and you invited me in, I needed clothes and you clothed me, I was sick and you looked after me, I was in prison and you came to visit me.

Matthew 25:34-36

Have you ever been a part of something that can only be explained as a "GOD THING?"

My husband, Mike, found out that a family in our church went hungry over the weekend. He talked to our Pastor, Phil Simmons, about how our church could truly reach families in need to prevent this from ever happening again. Through the efforts of many amazing people before long Cornerstone Assistance Network (CAN) was born in 1992. CAN started with a $30,000 gift from North Richland Hills Baptist Church. Now, Cornerstone Assistance Network is comprised of hundreds of churches, organizations and volunteers who are committed to this ministry of helping others.

There are so many different things God allows us to do at Cornerstone to help others. We have Christian Women's Job Corp which helps women gain skills for employment, the Medical Clinic, Case Management, the Creation Café that offers job training for those who want to enter the hospitality field, the Thrift Store where we are able to sell donated items at a reduced rate or even give to those that need help, housing for homeless and low income, and a re-entry program that helps those who have been recently released from incarceration.

I am Chief Administrative Officer and have a vast amount of duties that include but are not limited to fundraising efforts, handling the finances, human resource issues, reports for staff, board and grantors, managing building maintenance as well as managing audits. There have been so many times over the years that I have been able to see God show Himself mighty and big. Such as the numerous times I thought we would not be able to pay our bills and God has come through every single time ... no matter how impossible it looked!!

It is so amazing to see how God has grown this ministry from a $30,000 a year ministry to almost a 4 million dollar a year ministry. During our twenty-two years of ministry, so many lives have been truly transformed. It is always so much fun to look back and see the mighty work our truly good and gracious God has done. We sometimes get to hear testimonies from clients who will never be the same because of what God has done to help them here. There are so many days that we cry with tears of joy to see the gratitude and amazement in our clients to what God has done and it makes us overflow with grateful hearts as well. Last year we served almost 3,000 clients with over 45,000 units of service (food, clothing, gas, etc.). We know in our hearts that none of this could have happened without God!

Do you believe that God can use you to minister to others?

✝   Kay Doyle

105 ✝ ANGELS

Do not forget to entertain strangers, for by so doing some people have entertained angels without know it.

Hebrews 13:2

As she entered the room, I found myself silently laughing inside. This little old lady in an elegant feathered black pill-box hat was dressed for a formal tea party. I wondered ... why is she even here? Her grandmother type attire was unusual for the jobs available through our employment agency. And where had she come from? My office was across from the elevators, and I had not seen her get off the elevator nor had I heard the bell ding to indicate the elevator was stopping on my floor. How very strange!

Standing directly in front of my receptionist desk, this outspoken elderly lady immediately began asking me numerous questions. I was offended because it was my job as office receptionist to ask the questions and get each applicant to fill out important information on our official employment forms. However, I was amazed by her boldness.

The advertised positions available were clearly not for this person. I tried to discourage her but this lady with the sparkling eyes persisted, as if she knew a secret. Finally, I gave her a clipboard, thinking maybe this elderly woman could just complete an application and quickly be on her way.

Questions?? She was continually asking me questions while she was sitting in a chair that was directly across from my desk. The application in her hand simply did not seem important to her. I had others in the waiting room and no time to answer her endless questions. I politely motioned for her to complete the application thinking she would finish the form and finally leave me alone.

Suddenly, I looked around and all others applying for the advertised jobs had been interviewed and left the office. The two of us were alone. This little old lady insisted on showing something to me. With a twinkle in her eye, she explained that I might be interested in reading it. "The message in this book will change your life," she boldly proclaimed. I reached for the book and quickly thumbed through the pages. I was thinking that if I promised to read the book that perhaps this distinguished lady would be satisfied and just leave.

I turned away to answer a phone call; I glanced back only to discover that the lady was gone. Looking down the hallway, I saw no one. The elevator bell had not dinged. Where was she? Curiosity led me to walk down the hall and check-out the hall rest room, but no one was there. Where had she gone? Our office was several floors up so I was sure she had not taken the stairway down. I opened the door leading to the stairs, but I didn't see or hear any one on the stairway. Had the woman simply disappeared?

I returned to my office. The book was on my desk but the job application was on the chair where the mysterious lady had left it. Picking up the application, I was startled because no information was on the form. The book she left behind immediately became of great interest to me. As soon as I got home, I began reading it. This book was titled *The Late Great Planet Earth* and written by Hal Lindsey. I thumbed through the book and was startled because it contained information about the Bible that I never even knew existed. Frightened by many of the facts presented in the book, I hesitated to believe the information. I took the book home and read endlessly throughout the night ... I simply could not put it down until finished.

The next day, I gave the book to my fiancé, Nolan, and told him about the little old lady with the hat. He chuckled about the story and read the book with great interest. The message of the book began life-changing events for both of us. Together, we searched through the Bible to determine if God's Word really said what the author claimed.

Although we came to several different conclusions about some of the author's interpretations of the Bible, many facts were undeniable. The book described the end of time on Earth and how each person will be judged by God. According to the Bible, the decisions that we make will determine our eternal destination of heaven or hell. Jesus died for our sins so we could be forgiven and spend eternity in Heaven. For the first time in my life, I understood that God had a plan for my life. Also, world events were occurring in my life-time which had been prophesied in the Bible hundreds of years ago. And, regardless whether or not the end of earth happens during my life time, I must be ready for eternity.

Nolan and I began attending church and sought to seek God's guidance. From the point of reading the book, Nolan and I were determined to continue our own research to better understand Scripture. We read the Bible together but even more importantly we made a new commitment to God. Soon, Nolan and I married and made God the focal point of our life and marriage. Nolan began teaching an adult Sunday School class.

We had two children and raised them in a home where God was honored. Things weren't perfect! Our daughter was diagnosed with Cystic Fibrosis and we were told she would only live a few years. However, she is a college graduate and a teacher. A few years ago, I was diagnosed with Stage II breast cancer and discovered that God is greater than any battle we will ever encounter … even cancer. Our faith in God has grown with each challenge. And, we are thankful that God has been ever present throughout each trial in our lives.

Reflecting back now over forty years later, I know without a doubt what happened that day! I had always thought that angels appeared in white robes and a halo. But, I was wrong. The Bible says in Hebrews 13:2, *"Do not forget to entertain strangers, for by so doing some people have entertained angels without know it."* That elegant little old lady in a black pill-box hat was an angel manifested in a human form and she was not interested in finding a job that day in my employment office. Her job was to leave a book with a message which changed the course of my life. There was nothing magical in the book that she gave to me. But, God used this encounter with an angel to challenge me to search the Bible and study Scripture and to seek God's will for my life.

I believe with all of my heart that God intervened in my life that day. This angel who appeared as a little old lady was right; the message in that book did change my life ... forever!

✞   Marilyn Phillips

106 ✝ HE REMEMBERED

My night was dark and fearsome, My burdens heavy came,
Emotions rallied and screamed inside, Despair became my name.
When morning came I took my load of hopelessness and grief,
"There is no God who cares or loves, I'll never find relief."

And after trying every road that man could think or see,
I struggled, fell , and sobbed out loud, "Oh, God remember me.
I've tried it all, I've scaled the heights and all along the way,
I've gathered garbage, filth, debris, I need your help today."

And in my soul, a voice did speak with calm and strength and love,
"Just bring your load of rubbish, deep, and lift your eyes above.
Look at the cross and leave your load, now take in you My grace,
Here is My hand, My life, My peace, now We will begin your race."

I left my past behind that day, with faltering steps began,
To crawl, then walk, then finally run, the course that God had
planned.

Now when I see a soul in pain, I gladly tell my tale,
Of a God who loves, forgives, restores, a God who never fails.
I hope you'll come and join we two, the Lord and me I mean,
And find that life has meaning when upon the Lord you lean.

✝ ©Barbara Christa

107 ✝ TRAINING CHILDREN

Train up a child in the way he should go, and when he is old he will not turn from it.
Proverbs 22:6

One Christmas, shortly before mom died, she gave all of her five adult kids a special gift. She was a good gift giver. But this was a special gift. It had a message.

Mom gave us each a wall clock in the shape of the state of Kansas, which is basically a rectangle with the upper right corner chipped away. Different symbols of the state replaced each of the numbers on the clock. Since most of us didn't live in the state anymore, it was a sweet gift. And just in case we didn't "get it" mom issued this stern warning along with the clock, "You just remember where you came from."

The clock hung on my walls for a few years. Then the mechanism wore out and I couldn't find another that would fit it. So I packed it away thinking I'd find a replacement someday. Well, during a recent move I found an old box marked "KEEP." My heart beat a little faster as I unwrapped the clock – that special gift from so many years ago. It made me smile. I remembered mom's message with the gift and took a few minutes to reflect ...

My four brothers and I grew up in a small rural town. It was a safe place for children to grow up. All the parents in town made sure of it. In summer, kids would eat breakfast and then go outside for the rest of the day, only returning when hungry. We stayed busy all day exploring, playing with each other and with neighborhood kids, and playing with pets. But along with all the freedoms we had, much was expected of us. We were always polite to our elders; were in church every Sunday; and did lots of chores.

Mom wanted us to remember where we came from. Her Christmas gift was a reminder of our Kansas roots. But as I look at this clock now, I realize it was more than that. It was a reminder of the place where we were taught our values in life.

Those values included hard work, manners, common sense, and from the Ten Commandments: love God; honor parents; love others; tell the truth; don't steal or cheat; and more. And finally I think I "get it."

Mom knew that remembering the where, would lead us to remembering the what and the expectations to stay true to God's values we learned as kids growing up in Kansas. And it certainly did.

Are you taking the time to teach your grandchildren about the Ten Commandments and God's love for them?

✝ Anita Barngrover

108 ✝ SCARRED

The Lord has anointed me ... to give them a crown of beauty instead of ashes.
Isaiah 61:1-3

Screaming in terror, I stared into the face of a German Shepherd. At age eight I was no match for him, thrown to the ground, his paws on my shoulders, huge incisors dripped my blood.

I was afraid the dog was preparing to take a second bite when he was distracted by something. My brother had run inside in what seemed like micro-seconds, grabbed my father's bayonet war souvenir off of the wall, jumped on the hood of a car and called to the dog while waving the bayonet at him. The dog jumped into the air, barking and attacking the sword until the owners came running.

Whisked away to the hospital, I heard whispers about scarring and rabies shots. When mom fainted in the ER, I knew it was really bad! Over a hundred stitches later, I rode home with a sticker, grateful for a brother who cared.

The painful shots in the weeks that followed seemed far worse than I ever could have imagined. Worse were the reactions when people looked at me ... they gazed and quickly looked away. Before that, I remembered hearing people comment about my beauty. After the attack, the whispers were, "What a shame."

My face was a mess, and I had a new nickname at school, "Pizza Face." I should have been crushed, inconsolable, and broken. But, somehow, I was numb to it. Mostly, I was thankful to be alive and loved.

God turned everything to good through teaching me life lessons. I learned compassion, kindness, and the source of our true value. It has nothing to do with appearance. Like everyone else, our value comes from our Creator. *"For we are God's workmanship, created in Christ Jesus to do good works, which God prepared in advance for us to do."* (Ephesians 2:10)

Like my scars, pain or tragedies do finally fade over time. But the lessons learned from our trauma and the beauty God gives for our ashes never go away.

Do you have scars that only God can heal?

Prayer:
Father, Thank you for turning our trauma into triumphs and giving us purpose for our pain. Empower us to walk the path you've given us with joy and gratitude.

✞ Tamara Roberts

109 ✟ THE CROSS

Oh, Jesus, that you had to die for me!
This drives me to my knees.
It is more than I can bear!
So I surrender, shouting a thanksgiving prayer.

Flowing down from the cross were rivers of blood,
As your life ebbed away like a sorrowful flood.

These heartbreaking mental images at the cross,
Speak of overwhelming loss;
Being forsaken by Your Father,
Hanging, alone on a cross.

The compassion and love of a Great Savior,
Would be the only behavior,
To cause You to leave Your home for awhile,
To come to a place so dark and hostile.

So You came to bring the light,
To show us how to live and live what is right.
Is there any other way, You prayed,
But the Father asked and You obeyed.

The prediction of this great act of love,
Was written in ancient words from above.
No other way to save us from sin,
No other way for new life to begin.

Jesus, You provided the way on the cross,
So we will not live with overwhelming loss.

✟ ©Beth Peery

158

Ministry

However, I consider my life worth nothing to me, if only I may finish the race and complete the task the Lord Jesus has given me--the task of testifying to the gospel of God's grace.

Acts 20:24

110 ✞ SHARING YOUR FAITH

But in your hearts set apart Christ as Lord. Always be prepared to give an answer to everyone who asks you to give the reason for the hope that you have.
1 Peter 3:15

I encourage you to know as much as you can about the Bible. I have met people who don't believe in God, but they have knowledge of the Bible. They ask questions about things that are in the Bible that are tough to answer.

Some friends have an interest in the historical part of the Bible and ask questions that test my own knowledge of the Bible. Many authors share historical facts that can prove that the Bible is true! Knowing the historical context helps. For example, if you have knowledge of the first century and how tough the Roman empire was on Christians, you can understand how hard it was to be a Christian during those times.

One principle is to never get caught by the same question twice. It is a great way for God to design our personal Bible study. I encourage you to take advantage of your church's library, your ministers and Sunday school teachers. These people can provide studies to help you understand the Bible better. Also, read the commentaries and side notes in your Bible.

You will never have all the answers, but do you seek to learn?

✞   Rebekah Phillips

111 ✝ DIVINE APPOINTMENTS

Do your best to present yourself to God as one approved, a worker who does not need to be ashamed and who correctly handles the word of truth.

2 Timothy 2:15

Snow covered the ground, the wind was blowing and I was tired as I boarded the airplane at 6 a.m. that Sunday morning. Because I know that every Christian is to live "on mission," when I travel I make myself available to God to share His love with whomever He sends my way. That morning I prayed, "Lord, if you want me to tell someone about You, I will. But if you prefer I just rest and review my Bible lesson, that is just fine with me. I really am tired!"

I had flown to Kansas City on Friday, spoken at a ladies conference all day on Saturday, got to bed late and had to get up quite early to board this early flight to Dallas/Fort Worth Airport. I needed to be at my church at 9:30, and I wanted to arrive somewhat rested.

As I took my seat, I was delighted that only six other people had braved the early hour to fly on that plane. Wonderful! I had a seat alone and the other passengers were scattered through the plane. Ah, peace and quiet! Thank you, Lord!!

I settled in and spread my teaching notes in front of me. Just as I got comfortable, a handsome, older gentleman seated two rows in front of me turned around and asked, "And why are you traveling so early this morning?"

Uh oh! I knew. This man was my Divine Appointment. Knowing that, I carefully chose my words.

"I teach a large class of Single Adults at the church I attend, and I want to arrive in time to be with them." At the moment I spoke, the man's countenance changed and he became serious. After a pause, he said, "Single Adults …. Yes, that is important." Then he turned back around.

At that instant, my mind began to try to guess why he had acted so strangely. "Perhaps he is newly divorced … or widowed …" I could not help but wonder. However, I felt certain God had scheduled a Divine Appointment between that man and me, and so I waited.

The plane taxied down the runway and then took flight. As soon as the plane leveled in the air, the man stood, pulled out a photo from his billfold, and began walking down the aisle toward my seat. As he arrived at my row, he held the picture out and asked, "May I sit beside you? I want to show you something."

"Absolutely," I said aloud, but to myself, I said, "I have been expecting you, my friend."

The picture looked like something out of Bride and Groom magazine. There were four handsome, smiling individuals: An older couple — a lady and the gentleman next to me — and a young couple, a girl with raven hair in a beautiful white wedding dress and a California blond guy in a tux. What a beautiful sight! Each one looked radiantly happy!

My new friend began telling me a story. "That was the happiest day of our lives. My daughter and her young man had dated for five years, and we loved him like a son. Six weeks after the wedding, he was piloting a small plane that crashed and he died instantly. We are all devastated, and my wife and I are very worried about our daughter. She keeps saying she will never be happy again."

I asked, "Is your daughter a committed Christian?" "Oh, yes," he replied, "My daughter accepted the Lord at church camp when she was a teenager. Both she and her husband loved the Lord. And, my wife and I are Christ-followers, too."

In my lap were my teaching notes, and on top was a diagram of 2 circles, one inside the other, and a stick figure in the center of the middle circle.

I pointed at the drawing in my lap and at the Bible verses written below. I read them aloud.

"In the Bible in I Corinthians 1:30 it says, *"It is because of Him (God) that you are IN Christ Jesus, who has become for us wisdom from God—that is, our righteousness, holiness and redemption."*

I directed this man's attention to the stick figure inside the circle labeled JESUS.

"In Colossians 3:3, God tells us, *"For you died, and your life is now hidden with Christ IN God."* This means that when we received Christ as our Lord and Savior, we died to the old way of living and we now reside where?"

The elderly gentleman looked at the verse and at the large circle which said GOD, and responded, "We are IN Christ IN God."

I pointed at the stick figure. "This represents every Christian, but right now I am going to say this is your daughter. She is IN Christ, IN God. Can you think of any safer place to be?"

He looked at the drawings in amazement and declared, "There is no other place so safe."

Next I drew a cloud some distance from the circles, and I wrote "Storm" on it.

I wanted to make sure my new friend understood so I continued sharing, "Every life on planet earth experiences storms. Some storms we have created ourselves through sin, but oftentimes we have not done anything to warrant a storm. Sometimes we see the storm coming. Other times we do not and we suddenly find ourselves tossed about, unable to avoid the pain it brings. The latter storm is the kind your family has experienced. You did nothing to bring it on and it came as a complete surprise."

I wanted to give this man time to comprehend what I was sharing. So, I prayed silently that he would grasp this life-changing message.

Pausing to glance in his face, I explained, "But look again at the circles. See your daughter IN Christ IN God? Who had to give permission to let the storm touch your daughter?" (I pointed to the outer circle.)

"Why, it had to come through God's permission first," he replied.

"Yes, it had to come through God, who loved her and knew her before time began. Now look again ... who else had to give permission?" (I pointed to the inner circle.)

He looked startled and whispered, "It had to go through Jesus Christ before it could reach her. I see!"

"Yes, through Christ, who loves her so much He died for her. This tells us that God has a reason for allowing your family to experience this loss. He loves you and He will comfort you, but remember that He also has a plan that is a good one for each of you. You only have to trust Him to do what is best for each of you. Our LORD has promised in Deuteronomy 31:8, 'The LORD himself goes before you and will be with you; he will never leave you nor forsake you. Do not be afraid; do not be discouraged.'"

Tears poured down my friend's face. He pulled a handkerchief out of his pocket and began dabbing his face, but as he did, his eyes stayed fastened to the drawings. After a long pause, he ceased weeping and stood. "Excuse me for a moment," he said, and he returned to his assigned seat.

I saw him pick up a pen and a tablet, and when he returned, he handed it to me and said, "Would you write that down for my daughter?"

I drew the circles, added the verses and also some comments that I thought would help. Then I prayed for his daughter and for the members of both families who were grieving the loss of their young man.

The flight attendant announced we would soon be landing and the gentleman returned to his seat with a peace he had not had earlier.

How could it be that I would have been on the same flight as he? That I would have in my lap the answers he needed? I call such meetings "God-incidences," not Co-incidences. They are Divine Appointments scheduled by a loving God.

Do you know how to be prepared for a Divine Appointment?

✝ Barbara Christa

112 ✝ PREPARE FOR DIVINE APPOINTMENTS

Here are five suggestions to help you to be prepared.

1. Be living by faith in your own life, depending upon God in all circumstances.

   > **I Peter 3:15,** "But in your hearts revere Christ as Lord. Always be prepared to give an answer to everyone who asks you to give the reason for the hope that you have. But do this with gentleness and respect."

2. Study God's Word so that you can live a life that exalts Him.

   > **2 Timothy 2:15,** "Do your best to present yourself to God as one approved, a worker who does not need to be ashamed and who correctly handles the word of truth."

3. Receive good Bible instruction at a church where you will not only learn and better understand the Bible, but where you will also be encouraged and helped to live a life of faith and service.

   > **Romans 10:17,** "Faith comes from hearing the message, and the message is heard through the Word about Christ."

4. Pray about everything and trust God to answer your prayers with His best for you.

   > **I Thessalonians 5:17-18,** "Rejoice always, pray continually, give thanks in all circumstances; for this is God's will for you in Christ Jesus."

5. Look for God! He shows up every day but oftentimes we do not notice. See Him in the sunrise and the sunset, in the sky, in godly people's lives, in opportunities to live in such a way that others see Him in you. Don't miss Him and the opportunities He sends each day.

✝ Barbara Christa

113 ✞ HOW SHOULD I LIVE MY LIFE?

However, I consider my life worth nothing to me, if only I may finish the race and complete the task the Lord Jesus has given me - the task of testifying to the gospel of God's grace.
Acts 20:24

God has given you everything you need to be victorious in your life. Do you share your faith openly with others? Have you considered that God has brought people into your life for you to testify to them about God's grace?

"Testify" is a fancy word that just means to tell what God has done for you. Witnesses testify in court to what they have seen and heard or experienced.

Do others know that God has provided ways to be victorious in the challenges of life we encounter daily?

Do you want anyone to go through life issues or trials without God. Of course not! Our task is to share the saving grace of Jesus with others.

Have you shared the gospel of God's grace with anyone today?

✞ Marilyn Phillips

"But as for me, I will always have hope, I will yet praise you more and more."
Psalm 71:14

All eyes watch as the petite blonde confidently walks on stage. Rebekah is the guest speaker at the Christian Cheerleaders of America National Competition (CCA) in Chattanooga, Tennessee. This dynamic young lady proclaims that her strength for today and hope for the future is in God. Rebekah receives the *Christian Cheerleaders of America Courage Award*. This prestigious award is given for exhibiting outstanding courage in the face of extraordinary trials.

Rebekah shares, "I know that I have an incurable disease that may shorten my earthly existence. But, I don't worry about death. I focus on eternity. As long as God has a purpose for my life, I will be on earth. I claim God's promise that; *"I can do everything through Christ who gives me strength."* (Philippians 4:13) And when my purpose on earth is complete, I will go to Heaven for eternity."

Overwhelming emotion engulfs the audience. The audience weeps and listens to Rebekah's life story that is full of adversity and unshakable faith in God. Rebekah's tremendous testimony receives a standing ovation from over 450 cheerleaders who are there to compete for the national cheerleading title.

How can this young lady focus on eternity and have unshakable faith in God when facing an incurable disease? Rebekah has an unconquerable attitude toward a life threatening disease, Cystic Fibrosis (CF). The facts are brutal, CF is inherited and it is the most common fatal genetic disease.

At the time of her birth in 1978, Rebekah was not expected to live beyond the age of thirteen. Now, the average life span for a CF patient is mid fifty's. But, there is nothing average about Rebekah's life because the hand of God is on her. Researchers claim a cure for CF is near and we have even met CF adults who are fifty years and older. Rebekah experiences difficulty breathing daily. Although this devastating disease causes constant lung infections and frequent hospitalizations, Rebekah never lets the disease stop her from achieving goals.

As a cheerleader, this vivacious teenager's team won first place at CCA Cheerleader Camps for two years. During camps, the instructors notice her amazing attitude and leadership. Although cheerleading is physically demanding, Rebekah excels. She is accustomed to adversity. Some teens complain about a bad hair day but Rebekah often has bad lung days and struggles just to breathe.

I know first-hand about unshakable faith. I witness it daily! This courageous young lady, my daughter, is a constant source of encouragement. She continually amazes me. Although her appearance is normal, Rebekah takes over 100 enzyme capsules weekly to digest food and must have two hours of breathing treatments daily. Constant lung infections require additional treatments and medications and hospitalizations often.

Recently Rebekah is told she has developed diabetes as a complication of CF. Now, she must take insulin to control high blood sugar levels. I am devastated! I weep uncontrollably thinking how unfair that Rebekah must deal with two severe diseases. But, my daughter refuses to allow negative feelings. She says, "Mom, diabetes is just another disease. This is no big deal! We will handle this by focusing on God." And so, that is what we do each day ... focus on God. Rebekah continues, "God has proven over and over that He has a wonderful plan for my life. Another disease will not change my faith in God."

I wonder how Rebekah can continually give praise to God when facing constant obstacles?   Incurable diseases only make Rebekah more determined to live each day to the fullest. Rebekah's faith in God is unshakable and she focuses on a favorite verse, "*He alone is my rock and my salvation, He is my fortress, I will not be shaken.*" (Psalm 62:6,)

You might think that Rebekah is discouraged with the physical limitations caused by CF and diabetes. On the contrary, she is an inspiration to others through her faith in God and her courage in handling the daily problems caused by two diseases.

With much inner strength and faith in God, Rebekah continues to accomplish more than my mind can imagine or my heart dares to dream. She inspires her friends through her positive attitude. She always focuses on the needs of others. Many observe Rebekah's example. I have learned from my daughter that each day should be spent in a celebration.

Looking at Rebekah you would never know that she has an incurable disease. She is incredible and sets high goals for her life! Goals progress from high school graduation to college. With much determination, she continually succeeds.   Recently, Rebekah amazes everyone again as she crosses another stage. But this time, as a college graduate.

My daughter achieves her dream to graduate with a degree in education in 2002 to become a teacher.   Rebekah has always wanted to TEACH. She has been teaching at private Christian pre-schools since graduation. But, Rebekah has been a TEACHER all of her life. For, she has taught me about the importance of trusting God. And when I had breast cancer, she encouraged me to focus on God through the daily battles that I encountered.

Rebekah represents hope. She has shown others that the events in life, even diseases as devastating as Cystic Fibrosis and diabetes, cannot govern true happiness.

Regardless of life's circumstance, Rebekah's unshakable faith is in our great and MIGHTY God who gives hope in every situation.

Will you praise God today?

✟   Marilyn Phillips

115 ✝ GOD WILL MAKE YOUR PATHS STRAIGHT

Trust in the LORD with all your heart and lean not on your own understanding; in all your ways acknowledge him, and he will make your paths straight.

Proverbs 3: 5-6

I just don't understand why this is happening to me! Have you ever heard that from a friend? Have you ever said it? The Bible promises that we can TRUST the Lord. We don't even have to understand the events of today because God sees the big picture of our lives.

When facing problems, do you try to figure it out on your own? Do you weigh your understanding of the situation and possibilities that appear logical? The Bible encourages us to trust and acknowledge God. One meaning of "acknowledge" is "to learn to know."

Christians must put our faith in God's love for us and learn to know Him. If we do, we'll get a different perspective.

Are you trying to solve your problems today with your limited understanding or are you trusting in God for guidance?

✝   Marilyn Phillips

116 ✞ MY ADDICTION

I have what some people might call an addiction.
Sometimes I'm called Holy Roller, Bible Thumper,
or some other definition.

A great deal of the population is free of this addiction,
In fact some would call it a downright affliction.

Most people don't understand my condition,
They think it is superstition or a tradition.

I keep telling them about it and give them a proposition,
There is no other way to heaven – that's my position.

I try to live my addiction so others will come to the supposition,
That I follow a Mighty God who is worthy of admonition.

Still, there are those who have great suspicion,
That I have a screw loose and might need a geriatrician.

But I'm dedicated to my mission,
And will go to the grave on this expedition,

Worshipping the Lord my God with total conviction,
Continuing to tell others the Great Commission.

So, yes, I will say with complete admission,
I am souled out; I have a Jesus Addiction.

✞ ©Beth Peery

117 ✞ RUNNING THE RACE WITH PURPOSE

Do you not know that in a race all the runners run, but only one gets the prize? Run in such a way as to get the prize. Everyone who competes in the games goes into strict training. They do it to get a crown that will not last; but we do it to get a crown that will last forever.

1 Corinthians 9:24-25

When you are cheering for your favorite team, do you want them to win? Of course! It is more fun to cheer when our team is ahead!

To win a game, each team member needs to be conditioned and trained for the tasks. Football receivers train to run fast and out-maneuver the opponent. Baseball players constantly take batting practice so they can hit the ball precisely.

Athletes need to train for endurance to perform the entire game. We face races in life daily to listen to God and do God's will. What race are you running today? Are you conditioned for life's challenges?

We can train for life by reading the Bible and daily applying its principles. Are you trained in God's Word so you can run today's race?

✞   Marilyn Phillips

118 ✞ MY PRAYER CLOSET

There has been a change in me!
I feel as though I've been set free!

For a time, God wasn't number one in my life,
I had succumbed to sin and strife.

Prayer was not on my lips very often ,
My cold, hard heart needed to soften.

This went on for a few years,
There were empty feelings and many tears.

Then I remembered my prayer closet again,
This was my chance to let God reign.

To ask Him into my heart once more,
For me to open up the door.

This is where it's just God and me,
A place where broken and humbled I plea,

For mercy, forgiveness, grace, and love,
Although deserving none from above.

I can sing, praise Him, and worship, too,
Thank Him and confess sins He already knew.

I ask Him to watch over me,
And especially watch over my family.

Please save the lost people everywhere,
This is my most urgent prayer.

God never went away, you see,
The only one who moved was me.

Yet through it all,
God is faithful when we call.

He will never leave nor forsake,
So God sent His Son, our sins to take.

So if you're feeling lonely and blue,
You better meet God in the closet too!

✞ ©Beth Peery

119 ✞ LOVING OTHERS

A friend loves at all times.
Proverbs 17:17a

Every year at my high school, the Seniors went on a traditional week-long trip in March to the place of their choice. My class voted to go to Disney World. We were so excited about making final memories of fun before we went our separate ways after graduating.

About a month before the trip, I expressed my concern to some close friends about my medical needs. I required someone to do chest physical therapy on my lungs daily so I could breathe. This meant I had to bring one of my parents along with me. I was torn between two things - making my final fun memories with friends, or staying separately with a parent taking care of my medical needs. I wanted time with my friends with NO parental supervision. I was tempted not to go on this trip. I was frustrated that CF was going to stop me from having fun!

My mom told me that my friends offered to learn how to do the therapy so I could go with them on the trip without a parent coming along. At school one day, my friends learned how to do the therapy. Mom taught them how to "clap" on my lungs which was required to loosen the mucus in my lungs which was a complication of CF. They admitted that they were nervous doing it. I helped my friends by telling them to do the clapping harder or softer. My friends did a very good job during the Senior trip! I had so much fun!

What are ways you can show that you love your friends?

✞   Rebekah Phillips

But those who hope in the Lord will renew their strength. They will soar on wings like eagles; they will run and not grow weary; they will walk and not be faint.

Isaiah 40:31

Our grandson, Caleb, was diagnosed with Autism by his second birthday. We were all heartsick but there wasn't much time to be upset. We had work to do.

The State of Texas Early Childhood Education Therapists taught all of us about Autism and how to gently and steadily engage Caleb. The goal was to keep him from withdrawing further while at the same time attempting to entice him back from the place of solitude where he was. We prayed that God would give us hope and renew our strength.

This was a full-time commitment from his parents. Every waking minute of the day was an opportunity to use a method called Applied Behavior Analysis (ABA) to help Caleb learn to deal with his environment. We were introduced to Dr. Gordon Bourland, an expert in Applied Behavior Analysis who provided some private in-home therapy and a crash course on how to use ABA so parents, grandparents and an uncle would be consistent when interacting with Caleb. We were committed to battle this thing called Autism together.

As a set of grandparents who lived nearby, we were 'feet on the ground' relief. We helped with occasional household chores and grocery shopping just to give Caleb's parents more time for working with their son. We also provided some care for the new baby.

Our two other sons lived nearby and also helped. One set of grandparents lived out of state and helped with the search for answers about Autism until they decided to leave their home and move closer to their daughter's family. It was a total commitment from all of us.

We increased our knowledge base of Autism by attending conferences provided by Future Horizons, Inc., a comprehensive resource organization with relevant advice based on experience and cutting edge information. Our use of Future Horizons, Inc. products and tips on how to use Applied Behavior Analysis provided us with the tools we needed to be effective care givers for Caleb.

During this time my husband and I began staying with Caleb and his baby sister every Saturday evening to give our son and his wife time alone, without the stresses of home. Caleb's parents usually attended church services on those Saturday nights and spent time afterwards with other parents at restaurants. Things they were unable to do as a family, because of Caleb's inability to cope with the world.

We did not know how long the journey we were on would last. Would this be our 'normal' for the rest of our lives? Would we have enough strength to do all that was necessary, day after day?

There were no answers to our questions. But thanks to the prayers and encouragement from a group of friends and family we learned to depend daily on God for our strength.

Today Caleb is a polite, well-adjusted 13-year-old young man. God directed us and provided the stamina for all the hard work required. At school he's received awards for the top grade-level math score and is on the basketball team.

Caleb excels in all areas of school life-even socially. And my grandson does so with a great attitude. His determination to conquer new goals is evident to all. His parents, grandparents, extended family, and friends believe Caleb will continue to soar in life and we praise God fo his amazing life.

Are you facing difficulty in your life journey? Do you believe that the Lord will renew your strength and help you soar?

Claim the promise in Isaiah 40:31 today!

✟   Anita Barngrover

121 ✝ NEVER GIVE UP

"You do not have because you do not ask God."
James 4:2b

Blinking back tears, I peered between the bars. My brother, Tim, shared, "When I was showing off, drinking with my buddies and took that stuff, I never imagined I would end up here."

My brother wiped a tear from his eye. "When I pawned my kid's bikes the day after Christmas, I told myself that was the last time. Each time I failed ... I said NEVER AGAIN. But, I fail every day over and over. I'm glad I'm in jail. I've been a slave to this stuff since my first fix. I can't stop on my own." Tim was brokenhearted and so was I.

I gritted my teeth and dug deep for encouraging words. "I know. Maybe it's good for you to be in here. Maybe the Chaplain will help you find your way back to God."

As I left the jail, I bounced between grief and anger. A sob escaped my lips as I recalled the agony on my parents' faces. My heart cringed to see my family hurt from Tim's addiction, yet I knew I shouldn't stop loving my brother and praying for him.

I remembered a Scripture that I had memorized, "Come to me, all you who are weary and burdened, and I will give you rest." (Matthew 11:28)

Jesus' soothing words came to mind as I drove home. Determined to never give up, I'd let go and let God bear my burden. I'd lean on Jesus. And I'd do the only thing I could. I would pray. I asked God to remove Tim's desire for drugs and alcohol, to be surrounded by believers who would help him stay strong, and to become the godly man God planned for him to be.

Jesus' shoulder is big enough to cry on. He cared enough to give His life for our sin. He didn't give up on the cross. He never gives up on us.

Prayer:

Father, thank you for bearing our burdens. Help us stay committed to praying for our prodigals. Give us wisdom in how to help or withhold help. Empower us to never give up.

✝   Tamara Roberts

122 ♱ WHOM DO YOU SERVE?

Whatever you do, work at it with all your heart, as working for the Lord, not for men, since you know that you will receive an inheritance from the Lord as a reward. It is the Lord Christ you are serving.
Colossians 3:23-24

When we are at work, we try extra hard to please our boss. Our boss is in control of our paycheck and could determine how long we are employed. We want to be rewarded. If the boss is in the same room, we try even harder to good job.

So, how hard should we try when we are doing God's work? Scriptures say that we should work with all of our heart in whatever we do. Would that include Bible studies or work projects? Should you always do you best when you are helping in Vacation Bible school or being a counselor at a youth camp?

You won't get a physical paycheck for your work done on earth, but your account is eternal. Your reward is in Heaven.

Are you doing all tasks as if Christ is in the room with you?

♱   Marilyn Phillips

123 ✞ ARE YOU A MISSIONARY?

How then, can they call on the one they have not believed in? And how can they believe in the one of whom they have not heard? And how can they hear without someone preaching to them? And how can they preach unless they are sent?
Romans 10:14-15a

While listening to Chris Tomlin's World Edition of "How Great is Our God," I thought about what Heaven would be like. Tears filled my eyes as I envisioned a sea of people, not just from America, but from every tribe and language singing of the greatness of God. That mental picture brought back memories of the mission organization I was a part of during my youth. We sang "There's a story to tell to the nations" and the words have such meaning and challenged me. I had surrendered my heart and life to Jesus Christ at the age of nine and I told God that I'd be willing to go ANYWHERE He leaded.

Although God did not call me to serve Him on a foreign mission field, He did call our daughter, Megan. It was a regular occurrence for our family to share our faith story where we lived or on short mission trips. God began stirring Megan's heart, and she was burdened for people's souls and a lost world.

God was leading Megan to serve full time in Africa. She was excited to tell us of her news. My first reaction was, "Oh no, Lord, not halfway around the globe with its dangers and diseases." We encouraged her to stay home, teach kindergarten, find a place of service in missions here, and give generously to mission efforts. Megan's gentle response was Romans 10:14-15. Our daughter reminded us that many believers give money, but few "go" and she

MUST go and be obedient to the call. Megan added that if she were in the center of God's will, she would be in the safest place possible.

God taught us so much through our daughter as she served 8,850 miles away. Our faith was strengthened as we totally depended on Jehovah God to provide and protect. Because of Megan's faithfulness to our Lord and her desire to share the love of Jesus, many children and adults heard the message that Jesus saves. These new believers will one day be among the voices singing praises to our mighty God in Heaven.

Is God speaking to your heart about sharing His Good News? Whether at home or abroad, will you answer His call?

✝   Jane Weaver

124 ✝ FORGIVENESS

If we confess our sins, He is faithful and just and will forgive us our sins and purify us from all unrighteousness.
1 John 1:9

Have you ever picked up a rock and looked at it carefully? You'll notice rocks come in different sizes and different shapes. I usually "rock hunt" during vacations and I have a collection of my favorite rocks. I used these as an example of God's forgiveness recently.

I shared my testimony with a group of ladies called the "Lunch Bunch." I brought a few of the rocks from my collection to the restaurant and encouraged each friend to select a rock. The ladies examined the rocks carefully before making a selection and afterwards placed their rock in front of them. I surprised the ladies when I asked them to let the rock represent their sin and then pulled a LARGE rock out of my bag and stated, "My sin is bigger!"

The purpose of my testimony that day was to share with these friends how God has revealed to me that He is bigger than the sin in my life and explain God's forgiveness of ALL sin. So, I began my testimony.

I grew up going to a small church on the North Side of Fort Worth and Jesus burned a hole in my heart about the age of nine at a Sunday morning revival. I understood that Jesus Christ died on the cross to pay for my sin. I wanted Jesus to be my Lord. So, I made my Mother take me back that night so that I could walk the aisle and I accepted Jesus as my Savior and was baptized.

But, each time there was a traumatic event in my life, I questioned if God's forgiveness was "BIG" enough.

When I was a freshman in high school I was raped in my home by a boy that I liked, but had repeatedly said "NO" to. I was only 14! I never told anyone-not my parents, not my friends-until many years later. Feeling that I was ruined, I made some bad choices at age 15-16 that still try to haunt me to this day. But, I know God.

MY SIN IS BIG, BUT MY GOD IS BIGGER!

Before I married Dennis at the age of 18 in 1973 we told each other everything about our pasts, so we have no secrets. I felt that God blessed me when our son, Matt, was born in 1979 and was just the most precious little boy ever! Surely my sin was totally forgiven! I tried to be the perfect wife, the perfect mother, the perfect student, the perfect employee, and the perfect Christian.

When our son, Russell, was born in 1982 and diagnosed with Cystic Fibrosis later that year, BAM!, all of the guilt of my sin came crashing down on me again. Did my sin cause Russell to have CF? Was it my fault? For years I would struggle with this. But, God was directing my life. I was in wonderful Bible Studies and claimed God's forgiveness of my sin, but still it was a roller coaster of guilty feelings when life events were challenging.

When Matt was bullied at Middle School, I wondered, "Did my sin cause that?" When we switched schools and he and Russell thrived at Temple Christian School, I felt God was smiling on me again and the guilt subsided. During his senior year Matt was a class officer, played the lead role of Captain Von Trapp in *The Sound of Music*, and earned his Eagle Scout. Surely God was blessing me and I was forgiven!

MY SIN IS BIG, BUT GOD'S FORGIVENESS IS BIGGER!

Then, the unthinkable happened ... Matt took his own life on October 15, 1998! My heart was crushed! How could the sun even come up the next day, since the world was changed forever! BAM!, all of the guilt of my sin came crashing down on me again.

I asked "Where do you want me, Lord?" And I found myself in Bible Study Fellowship (BSF). I went through every study that BSF offered and God revealed so many truths to me through His word! I recalled how I was trying to be the perfect wife, mother, employee, and Christian in earlier years. Well, I realized during this season of my life that I was trying to do it in my own power most of the time, when I really needed to fully rely on Jesus! When guilty feelings and that heavy burden of sin tried to grab hold of me, most of the time I could use God's word and His tools to beat it! I was truly and forever forgiven and God saw my sin no more!

MY SIN IS BIG, BUT GOD'S GRACE IS BIGGER!

Years later, Russell married and I felt that God was truly blessing us and the years of ashes of grief and anger over Matt's suicide were turning into beauty (see Isaiah 61:3)!! But, when Russell and my daughter-in-law's baby died, I felt that God was slowly taking away people I loved because of my sin.

MY SIN IS BIG, BUT GOD'S LOVE IS BIGGER!

Finally, our beautiful grand-daughter was born. When I caught my first glimpse of this tiny one pound miracle, I felt that I had never seen a more beautiful sight and I thanked God for blessing us with her! She was born very pre-maturely and spent 127 days in the NICU. My wonderful daughter-in-law stayed protectively watching over her at the hospital until the day our grand-daughter was released to go home. Praise the LORD! God performed a miracle!!!

As I concluded my testimony with the "Lunch Bunch" that day, I asked them to look at their rock, which represented their sin, and think "OH, it is smaller than hers and surely it won't hurt anybody?" Well, that thinking is WRONG ... God has revealed thru His word that ALL sin is against HIM! SIN is against GOD.

Your rock may have some pretty characteristic that you like; it may look fun and interesting, but ALL SIN is UGLY to Holy GOD!

BOTTOM LINE

I like to pick up rocks, especially "Hole-y" rocks! It is fascinating to me how the power of water can, over time, erode away even solid rock and make a hole in it. Well, here's the GOOD NEWS! How much more powerful is Jesus' shed blood which immediately and permanently removes the entire rock of my sin for eternity!!!

Have you ever asked Christ into your heart to be your Saviour? Do you realize that Jesus paid for your sin and that God forgives ALL sin? Now THAT'S a miracle we can all use!

☦   Glinda Smith

When you pass through the waters, I will be with you; and when you pass through the rivers, they will not sweep over you. When you walk through the fire, you will not be burned; the flames will not set you ablaze. For I am the Lord, your God, the Holy One of Israel, your Savior.

Isaiah 43:2-3a

Regardless of what we go through, when we belong to God we have His promises and need not be overwhelmed nor defeated. He will sustain us. We may find ourselves misjudged, lied about, and mistreated in many ways. We will experience the losses that occur from living on planet earth. But we have a secret weapon that gives us the inner power to overcome – faith in the God of this universe who is our Strength, our Guide and the Lover of Our Souls.

Last week I was privileged to speak at the funeral of a twenty-five year-old mother of two. A year-and-a-half before, I spoke at her brother's funeral; he was twenty-seven and he also left two precious children behind. This Scripture brings to mind the change I have seen in the mother of these two young adults since the passing of her son.

She has shared that when her son died, she was "mad at God for taking my son." Now, looking back, she says God used that tragedy as a wake-up call in her life. She had attended church as a child, had even received Christ into her life, but she had married a man on drugs and took a road that spiraled downward for years. She finally divorced him in order to get her children away from addiction and to begin a new life. However, the consequences of her folly in their early years affected her children and she has reaped many sorrows. When her son died, the Bible class he and her daughter were attending ministered to her and her family. They brought food, visited her, and attempted to encourage her through those terrible dark days. Because of their love, she began attending the class. She has become a new person! This lady already had wonderful qualities – she loved her family, had a good work ethic, was good to people – but her life has been transformed and she has found God's peace and joy.

When the daughter died, grief struck hard once again but this time my friend kept saying, "God has been with me through this. He has gone before my family and met our needs." Quite a different response from when she was trying on her own to live a good, decent life. Why? Because she acknowledges Him as her "Holy One of Israel," her personal God. She relies on Him to take her through every trial and sorrow, and although the grief is real, He is sufficient.

We all go "through" hard times. When we are certain He is with us every step of the way, we allow Him to take us both through our circumstances and to the other side. And when we arrive there, we find ourselves changed, stronger in our faith and filled with the peace of God.

Do you realize that God is your "secret weapon" and available to you today?

☦   Barbara Christa

As a prisoner for the Lord, then, I urge you to live a life worthy of the calling you have received. Be completely humble and gentle; be patient, bearing with one another in love.

Ephesians 4:1-2

A prisoner has no choices. If in jail, prisoners must follow the rules. They get up, get dressed, eat, work, and go to bed following the authority of the system. Are you following God's authority?

Are you living a life that is worthy of the calling that you received from our Lord and Savior? So what would that life look like? The Bible describes it as a life filled with humility and gentleness and bearing one another in love.

Humility comes to as we see the greatness and glory of God and we are overwhelmed by our own weakness and sinfulness. Gentleness is the very character of Christ. We are patient with others as God is patient with us.

God's love flowing through us is what makes all of the other qualities work. Do you bear one another in love?

How are you showing love to others?

✝   Marilyn Phillips

127 ✝ TESTIFY

However, I consider my life worth nothing to me, if only I may finish the race and complete the task the Lord Jesus has given me – the task of testifying to the gospel of God's grace.

Acts 20:24

Breast cancer and my name should never go together. I felt energetic. I'm a school teacher and take good care of my body by eating nutritious food and exercising. My daughter and I swam over 50 laps daily in our pool. In addition, I get a pap smear, dental exam, yearly physical, and a mammogram each summer. So, no health issue surprises should come my way. Each summer, I received great tests results ... that is, until one year ... and I didn't.

Due to mammogram results, a biopsy was performed. And, it was discovered that I had Stage II breast cancer. Overwhelmed with unbelief, I fell to my knees in prayer. Surely, the test results were incorrect! I thought that God had a ministry for me as a teacher! So, how could I minister to others with cancer???

My husband, Nolan, and I prayed and agreed that whatever the outcome, God was in control. I knew that if I could trust God with my eternal destination that I could trust God with CANCER. I didn't know what the future held, but I knew that GOD held the future in HIS hands.

Surgery was scheduled and went smoothly. Many were in the waiting room praying that the cancer had not spread to my lymph nodes. Prayers were answered after the quick biopsy during surgery proved the cancer had not spread. I went home expecting a quick recovery. But, I was wrong. I missed the first few weeks of teaching school while recovering. I returned to school awaiting the official lymph node biopsy results which would determine whether chemo would be required. Finally, the doctor called. A new test determined that CHEMO was not required. I was scheduled to begin six weeks of radiation, Monday through Friday. The treatments were scheduled daily after school.

At first radiation didn't have any effects, it was only time consuming. However after two weeks, I developed a constant cough and recurring bronchitis and pneumonia. This left me so weak that I couldn't teach. I had to take off three weeks from teaching. My day consisted up sleeping until 8:00 and arriving for radiation by 10:00. Afterwards, I had to immediately go home and rest. My daughter, Rebekah, prepared nutritious meals and cleaned the house. My mom often prepared wonderful home-cooked meals.

Radiation treatments were a frightening time. I was fearful that my heart would be affected due to the location of the cancer. And when in the treatment room, the attendants leave and talk over a loud speaker. It was a "lonely" feeling while lying on the table and being cautioned to "NOT MOVE" because even the slightest movement would cause the rays to go to the wrong area. One day I realized that I was not "alone" in the room. I felt a presence ... and I knew it was God. I was not alone. I was overwhelmed with peace and tears streamed down my face. I was unable to move to wipe the tears away. I prayed, "Oh, God, thank-you for being here with me ... I don't want anyone to go through cancer without you. Help me have boldness to share."

I developed a painful strained chest wall from uncontrollable coughing due to constant bronchitis. And, I had to sleep sitting up. I was on an antibiotic and cough medications. It was weeks before I could breathe without painful coughing.

During this time of surgery recovery and radiation, my family, and sisters and brothers in Christ ministered to me greatly. I received flowers, notes, meals, restaurant gift cards, and powerful prayers. I was overwhelmed with this outpouring of love and encouragement.

Finally, the radiation treatments were over. On the last day, I went to my car and wept ... overwhelmed with joy that radiation was complete and I could heal. But at the same time, filled with compassion for others I had met at the treatment center because they had only begun the cancer battle.

I was able to go back to teaching my second grade students! Each day I was filled with a new appreciation for the gift of life. However, cancer still affects my life. I must go every six months for a diagnostic mammogram and blood work for cancer markers. It is always a great relief to hear good results.

But, I'm alive. But not only alive, I have a new awareness of life! Each day, I remember what God has done for me. I choose to remember the miracles in my life. I did not have a breast removed and I did not have CHEMO.

Now, after five years I am CANCER FREE. The Cancer Journey helped me to experience the mercy and grace of our MIGHTY GOD. I discovered that God is BIGGER than cancer! I have a new perspective on life and I realize that God was there every moment giving PEACE. I thought my ministry was being a teacher ... but, my ministry is sharing God's grace and mercy.

God has given me the BOLDNESS to tell others about my Cancer Journey. I am motivated to share about the MIGHTY God we have who is greater than any issues or trials that we experience in our life journey ... even cancer.

Have you experienced God's grace and mercy? Are you sharing?

✝   Marilyn Phillips

128 ✝ GOD IS MY ROCK
My salvation and my honor depend on God; he is my mighty rock, my refuge.
Psalm 62:7

I became a Christian in June of 1989 when I realized I had lost everything and had nowhere else to turn.

My husband and I talked often about divorcing. He didn't come home for the most part until the early morning hours because he chose to live a "party" lifestyle that I eventually wasn't included in. After we became financially bankrupt and lost our home, cars and everything of worldly value, Satan had convinced me that I had absolutely nothing to live for. (Even though I have three precious sons! Satan is truly the deceiver!) I felt that I had not only lost all of our worldly goods but also was married to a man who didn't love or even care for me.

At this point in my life and in this state of mind I had decided to commit suicide. I had saved up strong prescription medications for about seven or eight months. I had saved enough to fill an entire bottle … that would certainly do the trick. Every few days when I added medication to the bottle I always hid it in the exact same place. A wicker chest in my closet was a place that absolutely no one ever had any reason to look in but me. One day the decision was made to end my life that very day but when I went into the wicker chest the pills were nowhere to be found! I looked everywhere to no avail.

At that point all I knew to do was fall on my knees and cry out to God. I told God, "I have made a total mess of my life by doing things my own way. I am willing to give up my way and to try things Your way, God, if you will only take me and show me how. I hate this man I have as a husband, but I know in my heart that You don't like divorce. So, if you will show me how and work in our lives I am willing to stay with my husband and let You show me how to love him again."

From that day forward I have learned to trust God with my life and have learned that His way is always better than my way even though I sometimes try to take control again! That was over 25 years ago and my husband became a Christian two months later. We have fallen deeply in love and choose to live a life that we always hope honors and glorifies Christ. We have moved several times and the pills never showed up anywhere. I know that day in 1989 God touched my life in a special way and I never want to go back to that old, empty way of life again.

Have you ever been in a situation that was hopeless? God can be your ROCK and refuge today.

✝   Kay Doyle

129 ✝ THE END WITH A NEW BEGINNING

Delight yourself in the Lord and He will give you the desires of your heart.

Psalm 37:4

This verse in Psalm 37 has been fulfilled over and over again in my life and in our marriage. One of my greatest desires for my marriage has been for my husband and me to enjoy a ministry together.

Growing up on a mission field in the Pacific Northwest, I had a strong interest in missions. Several times my parent's hosted missionaries who were home on furlough. Other times we hosted summer missionaries. I was intrigued by them all and would sit for hours listening to their stories. Because we were on a mission field much of the emphasis of my elementary years was missions. We studied biographies of missionaries and the contributions they made in the world and the people groups they served. We learned of the hardships on the field and what they had sacrificed to follow Jesus. As a young girl I would often think about what it would be like to be a missionary in Africa and even felt the call to missions.

At the close of my elementary years we moved back to Texas and to our family. Once back we moved several times finally ending up in West Texas. With each move I moved farther and farther away from that call. However, there was always a draw to missions.

I went off to college and met my husband. We married while still in school. We graduated then moved to Dallas and then to New Orleans where our first child was born. Funny how a new born changes your life and a desire to be around family. We soon moved back to Fort Worth where much of my family lived. We planted our lives in a church that nurtured us in the area of evangelism which God grew into a plant producing much fruit.

Years passed, our second daughter was born (14 years later) and we both ended up in the education field. Teaching became our mission field for years. In January, 1995 John received his first invitation to serve with a ministry overseas on a short tem mission trip. Not ever having gone before he was to go and observe with the intention of doing one or two meetings toward the end of the project. However, God had something else in mind. On the first day of the project and at the first school to which the team was sent (about 2,000 students), John was the main speaker. The head of the ministry ended up in the hospital and John became his back-up. During that trip he spoke in over 30 schools. By the time he left India that Gospel message was locked in his heart.

Over the next few years John made many trips with this ministry. He went to India and Africa and always when he returned home I would ask him if God had impressed on him the need to start a ministry. The answer was always the same, "No, why would He have me lead a ministry?" The trips usually had a number of pastors and evangelists go. On two of the projects only John and one other evangelist went. It was this evangelist that ten years later contacted John under the leadership of the Holy Spirit to ask him to be one of the evangelists to go to Zambia.

John retired from education in 2006. He didn't know the rest of the story but God did. I retired in 2009. **The end of one career was only the beginning of the most exciting time of our lives.** We knew God was doing a new work in us, but what?

One Saturday morning as we were sharing a book by Bruce Wilkerson, *"The Prayer of Jabez,"* God had us stop and pray that He would extend our territory, bless us and keep us from harm. Just a few months later our friend Mack approached John for coffee. It had been some time since they had spent time together. It was during that encounter Mack encouraged John to begin his own evangelistic ministry. John came home and sort of laughed about the conversation. Here we were retired and the idea of starting something of this magnitude so late in life seemed ludicrous to him. Mack had also asked him to pray about going to India in January of 2010. Overjoyed that God was not through with him, John very quickly recognized the invitation to be part of the answer to the prayer we had prayed months before. So he went to India, then in March to Ghana. Soon after John returned from India, Mack once again approached him and said, "I am serious, you need to pray about starting your own ministry."

As we began to approach the March date for Ghana we both agreed we would move forward in prayer. Shortly into that process we felt compelled to begin the application process. We asked God to direct the process and open only the doors He intended us to walk through and close all other doors. So we started by naming the ministry and making application to become a legally recognized non-profit ministry. John went to Ghana in March to represent another ministry and by May of 2010 Evangelism Partners International was born.

Our first overseas ministry project was in October of 2010 to Ghana, Africa. Now God had opened the door for me to become a part of the picture. In January 2011, we travelled with Dottie to India to work with the ministry through whom we had been prompted to pray about starting a ministry. Before we left for India, John had received a letter from Leroy (the evangelist with whom he had worked 10 years before) inviting him to be one of the preachers on a team going to Zambia In June 2011. He did not respond to the request until after we returned home and Leroy called him.

We prayed and God seem to be saying, "Isn't this what you prayed for?" He went and from that trip our work in Zambia was birthed. John returned in January 2012, to work alongside a Baptist pastor in which the first church under our ministry banner was planted. A Project in June was planned and indeed God called five very special people to be on that team. Four of them serve on our board of directors today.

We knew God wanted us to work in areas where there were unreached people groups. The cities were evangelized but the rural areas were wide open for the Gospel. God caused our ministry to intersect with our now Zambia Coordinator, Iwell Phiri. Before he became our coordinator we worked with several other indigenous pastors to plant churches for our ministry. Iwell had been appointed Pastor of one of those newly planted churches in the east.

As we began to correspond with Iwell via email God confirmed in our hearts we were to work with him. In May of 2013 John and I travelled to Zambia to meet him and work with him. We instantly fell in love with him: his heart, his work ethics, his desire to see his nation and surrounding nations come to Christ. Throughout 2013 Iwell worked diligently planting churches, doing crusades, establishing Scripture Union Fellowships in the schools while teaching and training leaders of the churches.

In June 2014, we returned to Zambia with a team of nine Americans to work under his leadership in the southern part of Zambia. His reputation had proceeded him and he had great relations with all who came to know him and follow his lead. Iwell had been praying 5-6 years and asking God to send him someone to help him reach these groups of people. So from 10,000 miles away in Ft. Worth, Texas to a rural village in eastern Zambia where there is neither electricity nor running water, God caused our lives to collide for His Glory and His fame!

God continues to expand this ministry. EPI now has over 45 churches. We have been given land by the Mambo king (who is a lady) of the eastern region on which to build a training center. Iwell has identified and trained capable men to come alongside him to help him with the work of discipling and encouraging the churches in their growth. The ministry of Evangelism Partners International has been sanctioned and welcomed by the Mambo. She has introduced this ministry to many of her headmen (Chiefs). To date over 600,000 people have heard the Gospel message with over 400,000 responding to the Gospel. With 326 headmen reporting to her, the opportunities of growth are endless.

God truly has given me the desires of my heart and He has expanded our territory. The size of the miracle is God-size … why wouldn't it be? He is God and has had this ministry on His heart from before the foundation of the world. We are humbled to get to write this story of His amazing grace and love.

✞ Sharon Booker

HEAVEN
AND
ETERNITY

In my Father's house are many rooms; if it were not so, I would have told you. I am going there to prepare a place for you.
John 14:2

Forget the former things; do not dwell on the past. See, I am doing a new thing! Now it springs up; do you not perceive it? I am making a way in the desert and streams in the wasteland.

Isaiah 43:18-19

How do you feel about new beginnings? I mean "real" new beginnings! I thank God for them. I've learned to look at every new day as a fresh start, an opportunity to make better choices than I did in the past. I need those fresh starts and so do you.

I've learned that looking back and grieving over past failures or even holding on to past successes prevent me from moving forward. And I also learned long ago that the only steps to take are the ones God provides for us.

It wasn't an easy lesson for someone who had developed confidence in herself, who had been taught to "stand on your own two feet," and who blindly entered a new world where new temptations awaited. I had become a Christian as a child but in college I exchanged my worship of God for the achievement of goals I thought I could reach on my own. You've probably had a similar experience ... a period of your life when you were trying to find yourself and made bad decisions

When we drift, it is never toward God. Anytime we move toward God, it is intentional. And so I drifted, drifted, drifted until my choices were so obviously bad, I became miserable. After two years I would wake up in the morning and tell God I didn't want to live. I dreaded facing every day and I knew something was terribly wrong. At that point my prayer life became desperate as I begged God to show me what I should do.

I graduated from college and began teaching school, and although I knew my answer was with God, I didn't know how to get right with Him. Deep down was the certainty, however, that I had to get into a good Bible-teaching church.

One day I was driving my car, tears streaming down my face, and I prayed, "Lord, I am really trying to get back to you. I've looked and looked for the church you have for me and I haven't found it yet. I am really trying to do the right things, but every decision I make seems wrong."

As soon as I said that, a light bulb in my brain came on and the words that came with it were: "If every decision I make is wrong then I am not making another decision!" I immediately quit crying, looked up and said, "Lord, I am not making another decision. You're going to have to make every one of them!"

At that moment, I felt as though the weight of the world was lifted from me. I knew that was the answer: I was trying to run my own life, making my own decisions, and I had crashed and burned! It was at that moment I realized that no one can live the Christian life. Only Christ can. He came within me to live through me!!! Glory hallelujah!! I was set free.

In Galatians 2:20, Paul wrote, *"I have been crucified with Christ (I have died to running my own life) and I no longer live, but Christ lives in me. The life I now live in the body, I live by faith in the Son of God, who loved me and gave himself for me."*

That day I left the past behind, forgiven and filled with faith over Christ making my every decision! As a result, amazing things happened and are still happening. I found the church God had planned for me, met the finest Bible-teacher I have ever known, began to study and learn God's way for myself, and I began to experience life as God designed it to be.

Because He is the God of New Beginnings, our first waking words each day should be, "Good morning, Lord. What are my marching orders for today? I am at your service, dead to myself and alive to You!"

If you are trying to make your own way in life, leave your efforts and the past behind. Turn from your sins and receive God's forgiveness, made possible through Jesus Christ. He died so that we can have the life He described in John 10:10b, "I have come that they (meaning you and me!) might have life (eternal life with Him) and have it to the full (that means full and overflowing with God's blessings!)

Turn to God, surrendering control of your life to Him and relying on Him to make your every decision. You will find that "way in the desert and streams in the wasteland" that He has for you.

✝   Barbara Christa

131 ✟ HEAVEN IS REAL – SHARE YOUR FAITH

In my Father's house are many rooms; if it were not so, I would have told you. I am going there to prepare a place for you.

John 14:2

Heaven is real! Scripture describes a place for those who have surrendered their lives to Christ as Lord and Savior. God is there and we will spend eternity in His Presence. "The LORD has established his throne in heaven, and his kingdom rules over all". Psalm 103:19

Do you keep the information about HEAVEN as a secret? Or, do you actively share about the great and mighty things that God has provided?

We all will spend eternity in Heaven or Hell, but everyone doesn't understand that Jesus died on the cross for them personally.

Do you know if your loved ones are going to Heaven? Have you shared with others this exciting news? Are you keeping Heaven a secret?

✟   Marilyn Phillips

Let us then approach God's throne of grace with confidence, so that we may receive mercy and find grace to help us in our time of need.
Hebrews 4:16

Not long ago, one of my co-workers, was frustrated because she could not find a feather duster that she used in her work area. Other co-workers were trying to help. I have to admit, I was a little upset with this lady, because she seemed to get extremely frustrated a lot lately. I thought she must be going through something, but I just wasn't sure what it was. This lady had an aneurysm several years before, but she had made a very miraculous recovery throughout the years. My friend fought anger and frustration, and I don't think we could ever imagine what she must have been experiencing.

That weekend, following the feather duster incident on Friday, I received several calls, letting me know that my co-worker was in the hospital and had suffered another massive aneurysm. The prognosis was not good. Not long after, I received calls from other co-workers that she had passed away.

It was on a Saturday morning, and I was at our church Life Group when I received a call from her husband who asked me to say something about his wife at the funeral. I was surprised that her husband asked me to speak, but I knew it was from the Lord. At this point though, I just had no direction about what I was to say. I prayed and asked the Lord to show me, but I did not receive any direction at that point.

Saturday evening, we took our family out for our granddaughter's birthday. My son-in-law is the Pastor of our church, so I decided to ask him for his advice. I really needed it at this point. I asked him what he says about a person at a funeral where he doesn't really know what to say. He said I approach these sometimes by using, "What would that person say now that they are in heaven?"

It was like a light went on in my head and a "witness" was born in my heart. God had spoken to me through my son-in-law about how I was to honor Marge at her service. I was going to "interview" my friend in heaven.

I went home, sat down at the computer and the words began to flow.   As they did, God brought tremendous compassion and healing to any feelings of frustration or misunderstanding that I had felt at any time with my friend. I suddenly begin to remember the good things about her and begin to believe that she was experiencing God's presence and healing now. God's forgiveness poured over me, and I was able to think about "Interview Questions." God used this as a blessing to my friend's family and a healing balm to me. God's grace and mercy in our time of need is always available as we seek Him.

God is good, and He is our present help in our time of need. By writing an interview for my friend, it opened up many new doors of thought for me about how things are going to be different in heaven when we are "Complete in Him."

Have you ever thought about what it will be like in Heaven? Do you have the assurance that you will go to Heaven when you die?

✝   Donna Kirkendoll

133 ✟ WHEN I DIE

If we live, it's to honor the Lord. And if we die, it's to honor the Lord. So whether we live or die, we belong to the Lord. Christ died and rose again for this very purpose ... to be Lord both of the living and of the dead.

Romans 14:7-8

"I'm so angry at God!" my friend shared. She couldn't even put into words why she was hurt and bitter towards God. Have you ever been in a situation when you were angry with God and turned away from Him? Do you even remember why you were so angry?

These were some of the questions on a homework assignment for a class of fifty female inmates attending a class my husband, Jim, and I taught called CARE (Christians Are Recovering Everywhere) at Dawson State Jail. The majority of the ladies had responded with personal experiences involving the death of a loved one.

One lady answered, "I know the sadness and anger and grief that came from losing my father." Others shared that they felt angry after the death of a grandmother, mother, and aunt, uncles, cousins and friends. As I grow older, I understand that it is difficult to live into the "senior adult" years without experiencing death.

What concerned me most about the answers from most of the ladies was that I am going to die someday. It saddened me to think that my death could prompt anyone in my family or circle of friends to turn away from the God I love and serve. So, I decided to take action and help my friends understand that *"The Lord cares deeply when his loved ones die."* Psalms 116:15

For the ladies in our class, I prepared a Bible Study on physical death. I assured them that God can handle their anger toward Him. However, when we hold on to anger, it can turn to bitterness and a loss of our faith in Him.   Death is a fact of life, not a surprise. The scriptures confirm this in Ecclesiastes 3:1-2a, *"For everything there is a season, a time for every activity under heaven. A time to be born and a time to die."*

And another reassuring verse shares, *"Good people pass away; the godly often die before their time. But no one seems to care or wonder why. No one seems to understand that God is protecting them from the evil to come. For those who follow godly paths will rest in peace when they die."* Isaiah 57:1-2

Through my preparation and desire to comfort the inmates in our class, God provided the answers I needed to convey to my loved ones.

"Please do not blame God for my death when it comes. It is God's promise to me and I will welcome the time that I can join Him for eternity. The Lord has blessed us with our allotted time together on this earth and I am so grateful to be spending that time with you. Just remember that whatever happens in our lives, that God has a wonderful plan, and we can count on His promises. "

I have decided to share this testimony now so when I die my family and friends can grieve with tears of joy that I'm with my Lord.

Have you made the decision to honor God throughout your life?

✝ Sharon Willeford

134 ✝ ULTIMATE REUNION

For all have sinned and fall short of the glory of God, and are justified freely by His grace through the redemption that came by Christ Jesus.
Romans 3:23-24

Have you ever be part of reunion? Many have attended a five, ten, twenty and even fifty year high school reunions. The anticipation is great!

Recently I was sharing with a friend that I had attended a class reunion, and when I finished, he said, "You seem to have really enjoyed being with those old friends." I've thought a lot about that statement. Yes, I did enjoy it – in fact, I relished the opportunity. For weeks ahead I thought of who I'd see and what we would talk about at the reunion. I've always enjoyed my classmates and friends.

Once we were divided into separate classes and age groups, but time has a way of removing such insignificant dividers. We have all seemed to arrive at the same point: SENIOR ADULTS, one and all! Time has become all the more precious, for there is little left to waste.

As I've thought about our reunion, I realize that for some of us this was our last earthly reunion together.   The inevitability of eventually parting is in clear focus, whether we like to think of it or not. But friends, we can have another, far greater reunion to look forward to – and I like to think of it as THE ULTIMATE REUNION. I wonder if we'll all be there. Oh, I hope so!

Some years ago I came to a point in my life that I understood for the first time that I needed Jesus Christ as my Lord. I made the most important decision I've ever made, and certainly the wisest. I turned control of my life over to God and asked Him to come in and to use my life to accomplish whatever goals He had planned for it. I haven't lived a perfect life because sometimes I've thought I knew more than God did. However, those times didn't last long. It didn't take long for me to realize how foolishly we all live when we fail to rely on God to live both in and through us.

Why am I sharing this with you? Quite honestly, we should all be thinking about where we will spend eternity. Actually, it is time to face the realization that we don't have (as we used to think), "all the time in the world," and I don't want to miss this opportunity to share information that is so life-changing.

THE ULTIMATE REUNION! Who will be there? The Lord Jesus Christ and everyone who has entrusted their lives to Him. I have His assurance that I'll be present. It grieves me to think any one might not.

What about you? It's the best decision you can ever make! And think of the Reunion we'll have in Heaven!! Nothing on earth can compare. Won't you trust Him right now? He'll change your life for the better because He will give you His life, and it will last forever.

He has made everything beautiful in its time. He has also set eternity in the hearts of men; yet they cannot fathom what God has done from beginning to end. Ecclesiastes 3:11

✝ Barbara Christa

135 ✞ ARE YOU READY

Then I heard the voice of the Lord saying, "Whom shall I send? And who will go for us?" And I said, "Here am I. Send me!"

Isaiah 6:8

When we have asked Jesus to be our Savior, there are great expectations from God. To whom much is given, much is required. The great thing is that all God requires is that we be available to Him to become His hands and feet and His voice in the world. The empowerment is His. Although God doesn't send us all to a foreign country to be a missionary, there is much to do in your life that will honor God. Would you focus on these questions and ask God what He wants you do to?

- Do your plans include seeking and doing God's will daily for your life?

- God saved you to share your faith with others, so are you sharing?

- The only things going to Heaven are people, does it matter that others will not know Jesus unless you tell them? Make a list of those that God wants you to tell.

- Are you ready to go where God sends you? It could be to another country, but, often, it is a person in your family or neighborhood. Will you go?

- When you hear God's calling on your life, what is your response? Will you say, "Here I am, send me!"

✞ Marilyn Phillips

Contributors' Information

Anita Bangrover and her husband, Bill, live in Fort Worth, Texas near their three grown sons; three daughters-in-law; and seven grandchildren. Anita is a graduate of the University of Oklahoma and taught in Texas public schools for seventeen years. She is the American contact for New Beginnings Gospel Ministry, International, an evangelical ministry in India. She produces a monthly newsletter in addition to other duties for the ministry.

Sharon Booker is a retired educator of 34 years. She has a Bachelor's Degree in Elementary Education from West Texas A&M and a Master's of Library Science from Texas Women's University. After retiring, she and her husband John, felt led to begin a church planting ministry in Zambia Africa. They planted their first church in January 2012 and have planted 49 additional churches since that time. Sharon and John also serve as Volunteer Chaplains at the Tarrant County Corrections Dept. in Ft. Worth, Texas. They have two daughters, one son-in-law and two grandsons. Sharon is Co-founder of a group called GALS (God's Amazing Love Storytellers). Contact her at www.GodsAmazingLoveStorytellers.com.

Barbara Christa is a gifted Bible teacher. She has a Bachelor's Degree in Elementary Education from Southwest Texas University and a Master's in Education from the University of Houston. Barbara has been a church staff member for over 28 years in various capacities and ministers elsewhere, speaking at retreats and banquets, training teachers, etc. Currently, she is on staff at North Richland Hills Baptist Church as Minister of Single Adults. Barbara is married to David and they have one daughter.

Kay Doyle is Chief Administrative Officer of Cornerstone Assistance Network which is a ministry to homeless and needy in the Tarrant County area. She is married to Mike Doyle, Chief Executive Officer of Cornerstone Assistance Network. With the guidance and direction of God Almighty, Mike and Kay started Cornerstone over 22 years ago. They have been married over 46 years and have 3 sons and their beautiful spouses and 11 amazing grandchildren. Their lives are a true testimony to the incredible goodness and mercy of an amazing God.

Donna Du Frane is a RN who just returned to the Dallas/Ft. Worth area after being away for several years. She works as a Case Manager helping those with chronic and complex illnesses to aide in their recovery, to assist with advocacy and educate them with their particular illnesses/needs. She is currently praying about the next step/ministry God has for her. She has 3 grown children.

Carolyn Hedgecock taught middle school English and reading for Birdville ISD for twenty years. During that time, she wrote two collaborative novels with her students: _Locker Letters_ and _Camp Clearwater_, three short stories for the Western Writers of America, and numerous magazine articles. She and her husband, Joe, live in the Dallas/Fort Worth area. They have three grown children and twelve grandchildren. The Lord recently redirected her life to become a professional storyteller with a group called GALS (God's Amazing Love Storytellers.) Contact her for more information at www.GodsAmazingLoveStorytellers.com.

Sue King has taught piano lessons for more than 35 years and enjoys it very much. She plays keyboard in the music ministry of North Richland Hills Baptist Church, co-facilitates a weekly Bible study for women, and teaches children on the subject of prayer. Sue has been married to her high school sweetheart, Daryl, for forty-nine years and they have two grown children.

Donna Kirkendoll lives in Fort Worth, TX with her husband, Keith. They have two daughters, a son-in-law, and four grandchildren. Donna and her husband hike and backpack, and they love to share vacations with their family at Rocky Mountain National Park in Estes Park, CO. She also shares her gift of writing as she ministers to and mentors other women. She has written several poems.

Beth Peery is a freelance writer/poet living in Ft. Worth, Texas. She and husband, Ken, have four children and five grandchildren, soon to be six, all residing in the Dallas/Ft. Worth area. Beth has been an executive assistant in the corporate world and is now taking time to reflect on the incredible ways God interrupted her life with a journey to a personal relationship with Him.

Tamara Roberts , an author, speaker, and CPO of Bring Your Own Tiara™ is dedicated to encourage, equip, and empower women and girls of all ages. Over 100 of her articles have been published in periodicals and books including *Chicken Soup for the Soul*. She authored the novel, *Chronicles of a Warrior Princess*. A nurse by education, Tamara is a wife to Danny (Executive Pastor at NRHBC), mother, grandmother, and a daughter of the King of kings. Contact her at: Tamara@Tamroberts.com.

Glinda Smith is a Certified Public Accountant and has worked in the banking industry for many years. She has Bachelor's and Master's degrees in Accounting from the University of Texas, Arlington. Glinda and her husband, Dennis, have been married 40 years and enjoy singing in the choir at North Richland Hills Baptist Church. They live in the Dallas/Fort Worth area near their son and his family.

Lynda Swoveland was born in a small farming community near Waco, TX to two loving parents and grew up as an only child. She attended Baylor University and during her freshman year, married Duane. God blessed them with two beautiful children, seven grandchildren and seven great grandchildren. After retirement, Lynda's passion for working with women led her to be a volunteer for Christian Women's Job Corps at Cornerstone Assistance Network.

Jane Weaver is an educator in the public and private sector. She has degrees from Texas Woman's University and a Master's degree from Texas Christian University where she graduated Summa cum laude. Jane has taught Sunday School for youth and college students for over 30 years. She has been married to Thad for 41 years and they have two children. Jane and her family have participated in several mission efforts in Argentina and Japan. Her passion in life is to be ready, willing, and available to share the hope she has found in Jesus Christ.

Sharon Willeford is a wife to her husband Jim, a mother of four adopted children, a step-mother to three, and a grandmother and great-grandmother to many beloved children. Sharron graduated from Texas A&M-Commerce and attended Southwestern Baptist Theological Seminary. Following her retirement from AT&T, Sharon has spent many volunteer hours working with Senior Adults through her church. She has a heart to provide dignity to older adults, both in life at the end of life.

Scripture Index

OLD TESTAMENT

Book	Verses	Devotion
Proverbs	31:13-17	49
Proverbs	31:25-29	43
Proverbs	31:30	78
Isaiah	6:8	135
Isaiah	25:1	24
Isaiah	40:30-31	67
Isaiah	40:31	120
Isaiah	41:10	117
Isaiah	43:2-3	125
Isaiah	43:18-19	130
Isaiah	49:16	14
Isaiah	53:6	8
Isaiah	55:8	97
Isaiah	61:1-3	108
Isaiah	64:8	75
Jeremiah	29:11	45
Jeremiah	32:27	83

NEW TESTAMENT

Book	Verses	Devotion
Matthew	5:10	19
Matthew	5:14-16	102
Matthew	5:16	101
Matthew	6:19-21	70
Matthew	7:23	7
Matthew	7:24-25	29

Book	Verses	Devotion
Matthew	18:19-20	59
Matthew	25:34-36	104
Matthew	28:19-20	95
John	3:16	10
John	14:2	131
John	15:16	93
Acts	20:24	127
Romans	3:23-24	3
Romans	3:23	134
Romans	8:28	22
Romans	8:38-39	88
Romans	10:14-15	123
Romans	12:12	61
Romans	14:1, 13	52
Romans	14:7-8	133
Romans	15:13	16
1 Corinthians	2:9	48,69
1 Corinthians	3:16	74
1 Corinthians	9:24-25	117
1 Corinthians	10:13	23
1 Corinthians	14:33	12
1 Corinthians	15:33	77
2 Corinthians	1:3-4	44
Galatians	5:22-26	30
Galatians	5:22	31-39
Galatians	6:2	62

Book	Verses	Devotion
Ephesians	2:8-9	5,26
Ephesians	2:10	99
Ephesians	3:20	15
Ephesians	4:1-2	126
Ephesians	4:17, 22-24	73
Ephesians	4:22-24	71
Ephesians	4:29, 32	54
Ephesians	5:1-2	79
Ephesians	5:6-8	57
Ephesians	5:15-17	55
Ephesians	5:20	85
Ephesians	6:11-12	40
Ephesians	6:17	42
Colossians	3:23-24	122
Colossians	4:5b-6	94
Philippians	2:14	89
Philippians	4:7	13
Philippians	4:13	103
Philippians	4:19	25
1 Thessalonians	5:16-18	68
2 Timothy	2:15	111
Hebrews	4:16	132
Hebrews	13:2	105
Hebrews	13:8	27
James	2:14-17	50
James	2:18, 26	98

Book	Verses	Devotion
James	4:2b	121
James	5:16	63
1 Peter	3:15	110
1 Peter	3:15-16	100
1 John	1:7,9	87
1 John	1:9	124

ABOUT MARILYN PHILLIPS

Marilyn Phillips is a Cum Laude graduate of Texas Woman's University. She taught second grade students for eighteen years. Marilyn was a cheerleader coach at Temple Christian School. She is a breast cancer survivor and praises God for the journey! Marilyn also is a storyteller with GALS, God's Amazing Love Storytellers. Marilyn enjoys writing and praises God for her success. Articles have been published in national magazine publications including Guideposts, Obadiah, Home Life, Parent Life, and Living with Teenagers.

Six students helped Marilyn write the book, Fort Worth Kids' View. Authors were interviewed on TV affiliates of ABC, NBC, CBS and FOX. They also received a letter from President George W. Bush and First Lady Laura Bush. Authors also received letters from 30 state governors.

Eight book contributions include Chicken Soup for the Soul: Tales of Christmas, Chicken Soup for the Soul: True Love, Chicken Soup for the Soul: Christmas, Living By Faith, God Allows U-Turns: American Moments, God Allows U-Turns, Extraordinary Kids, and Chicken Soup for the Surviving Soul.

She has seven published books including: Cheering for Christ Always: 101 Devotions, Called from the Dust: A Journey of Faith, Hope and Love (co-written with Elizabeth "Moi" Lalnunmawi), Cheering for Eternity, God Speaks to Cheerleaders, A Cheerleader for Life, Fort Worth Kids' View and PRINCESS.

Marilyn has been married to her husband, Nolan, since 1972. He is a graduate of Texas Tech and an engineer. Nolan has taught Sunday morning Bible study classes for over 40 years. They live in Bedford, Texas, and have two grown children, Bryant and Rebekah.

For more information, visit Marilyn's webpage at www.mphillipsauthor.com.

ABOUT REBEKAH PHILLIPS

Rebekah Phillips was a high school cheerleader for two years at Temple Christian School. Her team won 1st place at Christian Cheerleaders of America (CCA) Camps both years. She was also co-captain of the dancing drill team.

Rebekah's life is a tremendous testimony to her faith in God. She was the guest speaker at the CCA National Competition in Chattanooga, Tennessee. After Rebekah gave her testimony sharing how God has helped her dealing with Cystic Fibrosis, she received a standing ovation from over 450 cheerleaders who were there to compete. Rebekah gained national recognition when she was chosen from high school cheerleaders across the nation to receive the prestigious *Rianne Ellisa Scrivner Christian Cheerleader Courage Award* for displaying outstanding courage in the face of extraordinary trials. Rebekah is vivacious and truly incredible.

Rebekah has Cystic Fibrosis. Doctors said that she would only live until age 13. Medical research, dedicated doctors, and the power of prayer have helped Rebekah achieve her life-long dream of graduating from college and becoming a teacher. Rebekah is a 2002 graduate of University of North Texas.

Rebekah is an avid reader and enjoys writing. Marilyn and Rebekah co-authored a children's book, _PRINCESS,_ about a little girl who has cystic fibrosis. She has an article published in _Chicken Soup for the Soul: Tough Time, Tough People_. Rebekah's book about CF is _A Breath with God: My battle with Cystic Fibrosis_. This book has over 50 Scripture references and encourages anyone with diseases to focus on God. She helped write a new book called Cheering for Christ Always: 101 Devotions. These books are available at www.mphillipsauthor.com.

HOW TO RECEIVE CHRIST

The Romans Road is a way of explaining the good news of salvation using only verses from the Book of Romans.

1) Acknowledge that you are a sinner.
   Romans 3:23 *For all have sinned and fall short of the glory of God.*

2) Know that all sin leads to death.
   Romans 6:23 *For the wages of sin is death, but the gift of God is eternal life in Christ Jesus our Lord.*

3) Know that there is hope through a Savior!
   Romans 6:23b *But the gift of God is eternal life through Jesus Christ our Lord.* Romans 5:8 *But God demonstrates his own love for us in this: While we were still sinners, Christ died for us.*

4) Confess your sins to God.
   Romans 10:9 *That if you confess with your mouth, "Jesus is Lord," and believe in your heart that God raised him from the dead, you will be saved.* Romans 10:13 *For, "Everyone who calls on the name of the Lord will be saved."*

5) Have a relationship with God.
   Romans 5:1 *Therefore, since we have been justified through faith, we have peace with God through our Lord Jesus Christ.*

6) Realize God's promise
   Romans 8:38-39 *For I am convinced that neither death nor life, neither angels nor demons, neither the present nor the future, nor any powers, neither height nor depth, nor anything else in all creation, will be able to separate us from the love of God that is in Christ Jesus our Lord.*

7) Say a simple prayer to God acknowledging your sin and that you deserve the punishment of death, state that you believe that Jesus came and took the death penalty for your sins, and because of your faith in God you know that you can be saved and forgiven and that you place your trust in Jesus Christ.

*Did you make a decision to
ask Jesus Christ into your life
OR
do you have questions about receiving Christ?*

Please contact Marilyn and Rebekah Phillips

http://www.mphillipsauthor.com

GOD LOVES YOU!!

THE GALS
God's Amazing Love Storytellers

Photography by Susan Bohanon

Our Mission is to refresh, entertain, inspire and encourage
by telling the greatest story ever told...
God's Amazing Love Story

The GALS (God's Amazing Love Storytellers International) ministry began in Zambia, Africa when Sharon Booker and Carolyn Hedgecock were on a mission trip with Evangelism Partners International in June 2014. During the mission trip, the men were scheduled to help build a church in the afternoons and Sharon wanted something more suited for the women to do while the men were working. After spending many hours in prayer, Sharon and Carolyn sensed the Lord was telling them to share about His amazing love with the women and children in the community. Due to limited resources and suitcase space, they decided to use storytelling as their vehicle because that was also what Jesus did. When they put all the words together, they realized they had an acronym that spelled GALS.

One by one, the Lord connected other storytellers (Marilyn Phillips, Rhonda Sparks, Terri Howell, and Tamara Roberts) to our group. We are educators, singers and writers who enjoy sharing God's love in creative ways. We are all active members of North Richland Hills Baptist Church in North Richland Hills, Texas.

MARK YOUR CALENDAR! GALS will perform the first Thursday of each month at the **Creation Café** located at 3500 Noble Ave. in Ft. Worth, Texas in Cornerstone Assistance Network. A donation of $8.00 to Creation Café covers the costs of a great meal and show.

It is our vision to share God's amazing stories wherever He leads us to go. We do not charge for appearances; however, love offerings are appreciated to help keep our ministry growing. No event is too large or too small. We use skits, music, drama, testimonies, video clips, costumes, and props in our presentations which are Scripture-based and revolve around ways we KNOW that God loves us.

We have numerous programs available and can create one specifically for your group or for the needs of your ministry.

For bookings contact www.GodsAmazingLoveStorytellers.com.

"The Lord's love never ends; his mercies never stop. They are new every morning; Lord, your loyalty is great." Lamentations 3:22-23

A Breath with God: My Battle with Cystic Fibrosis

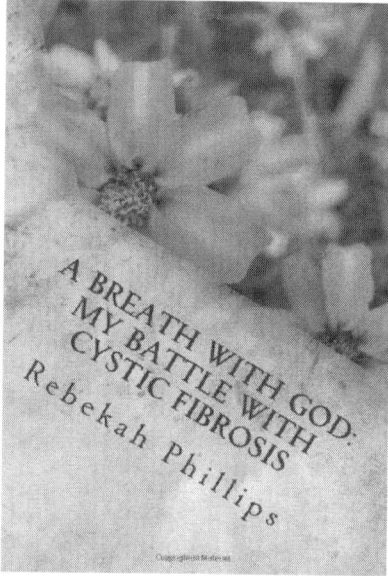

Rebekah's faith in God has given her hope and strength to fight this life threatening disease. Many have said this book was an encouragement in fighting the battles of life. Rebekah shares how the Word of God challenged her to never give up. There are over 50 Scriptures to encourage and give hope.

Called from the Dust: A Journey of Faith, Hope and Love

This true life story describes how Almighty God led Thang and Moi on a journey of faith into a ministry to India. God put an uneducated jungle boy on a different path. He now has a doctoral degree from South-western Baptist Theological Seminary in Fort Worth, Texas. He preaches to the lost and teaches lay pastors in India how to preach the Word of God.

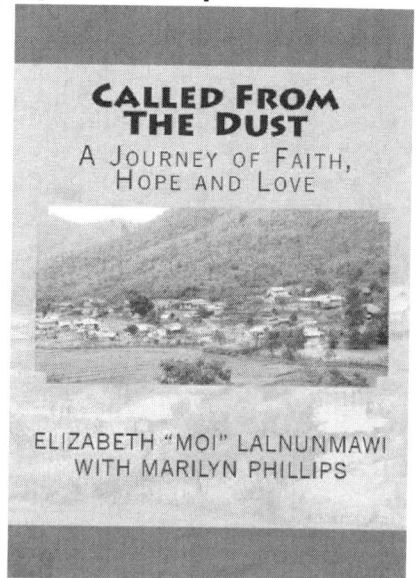

Books available at www.mphillipsauthor.com

TOUGH WORDS FOR A TOUGH WORLD

Practical Advice from Proverbs
Good advice can be tough to find in a TOUGH WORLD. We often look to many self-help books and sometimes we forget about the wisdom in the Bible. This book offers some Biblical advice on how to live wisely and how to avoid many foolish mistakes. All of this practical advice comes from the book of Proverbs.

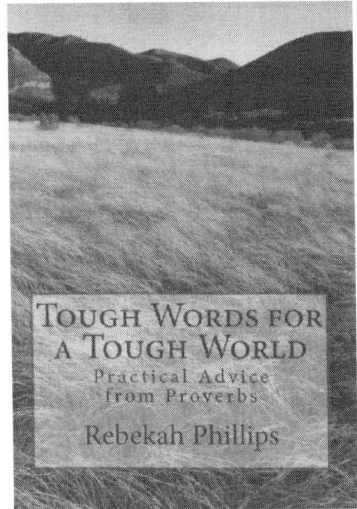

TOUGH WORDS FOR
A TOUGH WORLD
Practical Advice
from Proverbs
Rebekah Phillips

Cheering for Chirst Always: 101 Devotions for Christian Cheerleaders of America

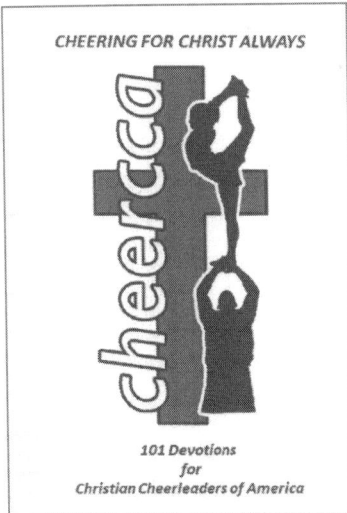

CHEERING FOR CHRIST ALWAYS

cheercca

101 Devotions
for
Christian Cheerleaders of America

This book is sold at Christian Cheerleaders of America (CCA) camps and it has 101 Devotions based on Bible verses to encourage growth in your Christian life and faith in God. Devotions will challenge you to deepen your relationship with God and share your faith with others.

Books available at www.mphillipsauthor.com

Made in the USA
San Bernardino, CA
29 August 2014